365 Affirmations for Hopeful Living

365
Affirmations
for
Hopeful
Living

PATRICIA D. BROWN

DIMENSIONS
FOR LIVING

NASHVILLE

365 Affirmations for Hopeful Living

Copyright © 1992 by Dimensions for Living

This book is printed on acid-free recycled paper.

Library of Congress Cataloging-in-Publication Data

Brown, Patricia D., 1953–
  365 affirmations for hopeful living / Patricia D. Brown.
    p.   cm.
  Includes index.
  ISBN 0-687-41889-5 (alk. paper)
  1. Hope—Religious aspects—Christianity—Prayer-books and devotions—English. 2. Devotional calendars. I. Title.
II. Title: Three hundred sixty-five affirmations for hopeful living.
BV4638.B697   1992
242'.2—dc20   92–18261
                                                            CIP

Scripture quotations are from the New Revised Standard Version Bible, copyright © 1989 by the Division of Christian Education of the National Council of the Churches of Christ in the United States of America, and are used by permission.

Meditations for March and April are adapted from *The Sanctuary for Lent 1992*, Patricia D. Brown, © 1992 by Abingdon Press, and are used by permission.

95 96 97 98 99 00 01 02 03 04 — 10 9 8 7 6 5 4 3

MANUFACTURED IN THE UNITED STATES OF AMERICA

──ACKNOWLEDGMENTS──

*T*his book is precious to me because it reflects my own story and the journey of many other women and men who have shared joys and sorrows. Some have been my mentors; others have allowed me to be a guide in their discipleship journey. Through these interactions in community we have found healing.

I am thankful for all the people who have supported me in my Christian journey, bringing me to this day to write these affirmations. Special thanks to my family: Dale, my spouse, for his rich supply of love, tireless support, and editing skills; Christian, my teenage son, who kept me honest; and Stephen, my five-year-old, who reminded me to play. Their support through this book meant everything. My thanks to my home pastor and friend, David Keller, whose faith in me keeps me keeping on; to Carola Beasley-Topliffe, Ira and Joyce Goldstein, Cynthia Stine, Allen Hulslander, Beth Miller, and other colleagues whose feedback, insights, and support I gratefully acknowledge; to Ron Patterson, who shared my vision and encouraged me to write; and, finally, to my editor, Sally Sharpe, whose patience and insight through the drafts have enriched this book tremendously.

My thanks go to many. My thanks and praise go to God.

INTRODUCTION

*A*ffirmations for hopeful living are a personal "YES! NOW!" to God's movement in our lives. They are powerful, positive statements that declare how we want to live as disciples of Jesus Christ. When we allow ourselves to say "YES!" to the work of the Holy Spirit, we then are able to change and move on. Whatever our circumstance, we all are in need of God's grace. God's grace, and our efforts to acknowledge and employ that grace, are what affirmations are all about.

As we read or write affirmations, we establish a dialogue with self, God, and others. We ask, "What is it that is emerging from within me?" We search our lifelong dreams, our intuitions, and our deepest desires to build affirmations about our lives as disciples. Through these emerging affirmations we go to God with a new attitude of prayer. We are ready to listen and act. We are open in new ways to God's purposeful work in our lives.

This book is written for those who want to replace their critical inner dialogue and prayer with positive, life-giving language. The messages we give ourselves and the conversations we pray are crucial in determining our attitude, outlook, behavior, and path. There are parts of ourselves we dislike. We can begin to change those parts by conversing, praying, and living in new ways. There are other parts of ourselves we'd like to enhance. These, too, need to be lifted up in prayer and presented to God, who will strengthen us and use our gifts. Setting aside time each day to form images of ourselves behaving as Christian disciples is an important beginning.

Using affirmations as guides, we pray to change old messages and reverse patterns that no longer fit as we accept God's unconditional love and forgiveness. Along with our love for God and neighbor, we also seek to love ourselves. This love of self is not to be mistaken as narcissistic or selfish. Instead, it is a genuine concern for ourselves which enables us to extend our love to God and others. We begin to draw a new self-portrait revealing a member of God's community who is healthy, whole, and Christ-centered.

Here are a few practical guidelines for using the affirmations in this book:

❦ Remember that affirmations are communicated in the present tense. They are positive statements written and spoken in the first person singular. Never say "I can" but "I am."

❧ If you are not already part of a Christian community, seek a fellowship of believers in which you can share when appropriate. A Christian community provides you with a place for support and reflection as you work to put your affirmations into action. Remember, no one grows in isolation.

❧ To use these affirmations effectively, read each message aloud. You may need to repeat it several times. Reflect on its meaning and then form it into a prayer. Beware of negative thoughts which try to take over or statements which negate your value, worth, or esteem as a person of God.

❧ Recognize that some affirmations will not catch your attention or seem to fit, because they are not relevant to your life now. Also, remember that no one affirmation can be complete in and of itself. Each touches only a small part of your total. Everything about your specific situation cannot be covered in one daily affirmation.

❧ For use in Bible study or fellowship groups, choose one or more affirmations and read aloud to the entire group. Each person can then reflect on its meaning and how it speaks to her or his life. These are not to be sessions that dwell on the intense past of despair and pain. Instead, they are opportunities for sustaining power, new hope, and energy for the discipleship walk in community.

My hope is that this book will be a catalyst for all followers of Christ who are on the road of discipleship. May it be a new beginning for those who are called of God and ready to accept the peace, joy, and light offered in Jesus.

JANUARY 1   HOPE

When Jesus saw the crowds, he went up the mountain. . . . Then he began to speak, and taught them.
—Matthew 5:1-2

Jesus has words to speak to me. I am to listen and learn in these days. Today I make a fresh start. This day is like a blank sheet of paper on which my Lord and I can write new ways of being and doing in the world. I will write about what I lovingly wish in my relationship with Jesus, with myself, and with others.

I expect this day to be a day of healing, to feel energizing health pulsing through me. I expect today to be a day of joy, in which I will be freed from anxieties. I expect this day to be a day of love, with satisfying relationships. I expect today, and each day, to be a time of renewal and a deepening understanding of myself as a disciple of Jesus Christ.

I welcome this new season, this new day, and this new me.

JANUARY 2   SPIRITUAL POWERS

Now to him who by the power at work within us is able to accomplish abundantly far more than all we can ask or imagine, to him be glory in the church and in Christ Jesus to all generations, forever and ever. Amen.
—Ephesians 3:20-21

There is a strong power at work in me today. Its presence empowers me to do far more in my life than I ever dreamed possible. If a situation makes me feel low, I remember that the difficult time will not last forever. In Christ I have the power to live through the difficulty, knowing that good times will return.

I choose to live my life to its fullest. Each new day brings opportunities to stretch my horizons, try new experiences, and assert my power. In the past I limited my own vision of what I thought was possible. Yet in Christ these barriers are torn down so that I can be free to dream and envision. I am thankful that through Christ I can accomplish far more than I ever thought possible.

Today I choose to live my life centered in the power of Jesus Christ.

—— ❦ ——

JANUARY 3   GOALS

This one thing I do: forgetting what lies behind and straining forward to what lies ahead, I press on toward the goal for the prize of the heavenly call of God in Christ Jesus.   —Philippians 3:13b-14

Today I will begin my journey with a single step. I will take the time to think about my goals and plans and how they can be reached. I will reflect on what I want in my relationships. I will pray concerning what I need spiritually, emotionally, and physically as I work toward one of my goals.

I need to remember that my goals are set in accordance with God's will for my life. So I ask, "What does God want me to achieve?" or "What does God have in store for me?" I am able to leave the past in the past and strain forward to the future, to God's call, and to purpose in my life.

Yesterday I blocked my own and God's efforts. Today I choose my direction and find strength to take that next step toward achieving my goal.

I choose one act today which moves me one step closer to my goal.

※

JANUARY 4   DECISION

I know your works; you are neither cold nor hot. I wish that you were either cold or hot. So, because you are lukewarm, and neither cold nor hot, I am about to spit you out of my mouth.   —Revelation 3:15-16

Today I move out of my mediocrity and lukewarmness in decision making. I will throw off my feelings of powerlessness and apathy. The time has come to let go, begin to forgive, and move on.

My life does have importance and purpose. I am not a lukewarm person, but I am a person who is able to make clear, purposeful choices. I am free of the numbness that kept me from taking action. I look in each new day for possibilities to make decisions that will give me fresh direction.

Today, with the help of God, I shake off my apathy, take my stand, make my statement, and hold firm in my convictions.

JANUARY 5   DISCIPLESHIP

But now that faith has come, we are no longer subject to a disciplinarian, for in Christ Jesus you are all children of God through faith. As many of you as were baptized into Christ have clothed yourselves with Christ.   —*Galatians 3:25-27*

The "clothes" I wear show the new life I've found, for they are a new way of living. Today, as a child of God, I choose "clothes" that suit the new me. The vibrant clothes I wear are shown through words Jesus would choose for me: "I can," "I will," "I do." These words help me live in self-affirming ways.

Baptism is evidence of Christ's love for me. The water of baptism washes away the sinfulness that keeps me trudging along joylessly. In Christ I am clean and fresh, ready to face the day.

I clothe myself in beautiful fabrics which display that I am a child of God in Christ.

JANUARY 6   *DISCIPLESHIP*

Then Jesus told his disciples, "If any want to become my followers, let them deny themselves and take up their cross and follow me."   —Matthew 16:24

"Well, here I am, Lord. You said to take up your cross and follow you, and I'm here to do it. It's not easy, you know, this self-denial thing. But I've come to pick up my cross."

"Excuse me, Lord, but there doesn't seem to be much of a selection here. Only these rough, coarse, wooden ones. I mean, that could hurt! I was thinking of something a bit more convenient, perhaps smaller."

"What's that? It's either one of these or forget the whole thing? Being a disciple is challenging and exciting, and I want to do it. But . . . "

"OK, Lord. I know I can't do it alone, but you have promised to be there for me when I need your help. And that's enough."

The cross that I am called to pick up is not an easy one, but I pick it up with the help of God and go on.

JANUARY 7   TRANSFORMATION

*"Very truly, I tell you, no one can see the kingdom of
God without being born from above."*   —*John 3:3*

In the morning as I rise, I begin life anew. I
have been born of God, and God's spirit is
within me. I start this day with a fresh outlook. I separate myself from the stresses and
burdens of yesterday and greet this new day
with renewed energy.

I am born again and again and again. God is
not finished with me yet. I am always on my
way to becoming the person God wants me to
be. Being born again, I can now envision and
be part of God's reign here on Earth.

Today is a turning point and the beginning
of a new season in my walk with Christ. I
know I don't have to change completely
today, but I can take the risk to change in
some small way.

**Today I see myself function in the world, born
anew.**

JANUARY 8   HOPE

For in hope we were saved. Now hope that is seen is not hope. For who hopes for what is seen? But if we hope for what we do not see, we wait for it with patience.   —Romans 8:24-25

I am a person who lives in hope. My hope allows me to dream dreams and envision coming realities. With hope for the future, I can concentrate on clearly defining what I want in life. I take action to bring my visualizations into reality.

In the past I hoped for magical solutions to my problems. I dreaded the future and wished for the next day or the next week or the next year to be better. Today I claim the hope I have in Christ. I live as a hope-filled person. I act in ways to make my hopes become realities.

As I welcome the challenges today brings, I begin to fulfill my hope in one small step.

May the God of hope fill you with all joy and peace in believing, so that you may abound in hope by the power of the Holy Spirit. —Romans 15:13

I have discovered that life is joyful, and that joy and peace go together! At one time I lived sadly in darkness, but now I have entered the light of joy. I am free to laugh, to sing, and to play. I receive true joy in my day when I remember that God loves me.

Because I have joy in knowing God, I have the strength to face the world. I have confidence that's infectious. This day I turn to the joy of laughter because I have good news to share. I speak and think joyously in my life. God wants me to be a joyful person and to live jubilantly.

By the power of the Holy Spirit, I am filled with the energy of hope, the peace of believing, and the joy of God.

Rejoice in the Lord always; again I will say, Rejoice.
—*Philippians 4:4*

Today I can rejoice in the quiet strength that surrounds me. I am relaxed and serene. I feel no stress or pressure. I live a joyous existence knowing that God enfolds me. I have the resources I need to meet whatever difficulties I encounter.

For years I was the one who took care of every emergency and crisis. I looked after everyone's problems. If it was broken, I could fix it. Each day my resentment grew as I waited for the time to come when I would be cared for. What an exhausting way to live!

Now I want to live as a person of joy. Again and again I rejoice that I can help in realistic ways and not expect the impossible from myself. I choose to live with joy in the land of possibilities.

Today I realize that God intends for me to live a joyful life, free from compulsive ways.

JANUARY 11   GIVING

"As you go, proclaim the good news, 'The kingdom of heaven has come near.' Cure the sick, raise the dead, cleanse the lepers, cast out demons. You received without payment; give without payment."

—*Matthew 10:7-8*

Jesus tells me to give of my time, talents, and possessions to help other people. But I am not to do good for others because I believe I will be repaid. Jesus tells me to give to others because God gave first to me without expecting payment.

Yesterday I did favors for friends, relatives, or even strangers because I wanted to coerce them into doing something for me. I wanted to be repaid with their admiration or attention. I now know that I do not always need to get something in return for my giving.

Today I give because I enjoy giving . . . with no strings attached. Jesus has blessed me with abilities to be used in the healing of myself and others. I give of my abilities and talents freely.

I am a good person, and I give out of that goodness.

—— ❦ ——

JANUARY 12   HEALTH

There appeared a woman with a spirit that had crippled her for eighteen years. . . . When Jesus saw her, he called her over and said, "Woman, you are set free from your ailment."   —Luke 13:11-12

The woman in the Bible story was freed from her ailment to live in good health. That is God's desire for me, too. I long to hear Jesus say: "*You* are set free from your ailment." Yet, like the woman who came in faith, I, too, have a role to play in my own healing.

Part of being a follower of Jesus Christ is to nurture myself. This means taking good care of my physical self. Today I will nurture my body in healthy ways. I will eat nutritious food, enjoy some exercise, and rest when I need to rest. I feel good about my physical identity and it shows in how I take care of my health. I am joyous in my good health.

I take good care of my body, which is a gift from God.

Or do you not know that your body is a temple of the Holy Spirit within you, which you have from God, and that you are not your own? For you were bought with a price; therefore glorify God in your body.
                         —1 Corinthians 6:19-20

Today I recognize my body as a gift from God. I breathe deeply, conscious that the Holy Spirit lives within me. I adopt habits of good health that will keep me vital and energetic. My new patterns of healthy living are satisfying to me—mentally and spiritually as well as physically.

I do not expect to change all my old habits overnight. Moderation, not perfection, is what I ask from myself today. I choose one act of health today. I can take a walk, eat a salad, or get enough rest. I look forward to a healthy body and will make an effort to change.

I recognize that my physical health is an expression of what God intends.

JANUARY 14   PEACE

"Peace I leave with you; my peace I give to you. I do not give to you as the world gives. Do not let your hearts be troubled, and do not let them be afraid."
—*John 14:27*

Jesus promises that the Holy Spirit will impart peace to all disciples. It is a peace that I long for and must have in my life. This peace is one the "world" cannot give me. I seek God for this peace. I do not depend on other people or things to give me contentment. I have all the peace I need because the Holy Spirit lives within me.

Inner disruption and dissension have no place if I am to conduct my life in harmony and balance. At this moment I will empty myself of turbulent thoughts and allow peace to fill me. When I am filled with God's peace there is order within me, even in the midst of difficult circumstances.

Today, with the power of the Holy Spirit, I am centered in harmony to remain in peace in every circumstance I encounter.

—❦—

JANUARY 15   *PEACE*

Do not worry about anything, but in everything by prayer and supplication with thanksgiving let your requests be made known to God. And the peace of God, which surpasses all understanding, will guard your hearts and your minds in Christ Jesus.
        —Philippians 4:6-7

At this moment I have quieted the storms in my thoughts and invited peace to fill the calm. I know God's power lies in the peacefulness within me. When I am balanced and centered, I am able to think clearly and to see life in positive ways. When I am a center for Jesus and what he wants for my life, I am at peace with myself and can see clearly my purpose in life.

In prayer I ask God to release me from self-defeating ways of thinking and living so harmony can be restored to my day. How God's peace comes to me is a mystery, but it is a mystery for which I am thankful. God watches over and guards me so I do not need to worry or fear.

Today I pray for God to keep me centered and at peace.

JANUARY 16   SPIRITUAL POWERS

God did not give us a spirit of cowardice, but rather a spirit of power and of love and of self-discipline.
—2 Timothy 1:7

Because God is present, I do not fear the unknown of today. I choose to live my life with the power that God gives.

I have a spirit of power that gives me a new perspective on life. With this new perspective I am able to be bold and decisive in my actions. I have a spirit of love that pushes me to grow and become fulfilled. I have a spirit of self-discipline and self-control that influences my reactions to events and people.

With God's power, I move forward in fulfilling my potential. Today I live in a spirit of power, love, and self-control.

JANUARY 17   THANKFULNESS

Be filled with the Spirit, as you sing psalms and hymns and spiritual songs among yourselves, singing and making melody to the Lord in your hearts, giving thanks to God the Father at all times and for everything in the name of our Lord Jesus Christ.

—Ephesians 5:18b-20

Today I give thanks for my life. I know the experiences that come today will add to my knowledge and I will grow in my understanding. I have a mission in partnership with God and I will actively work to engage in this mission. I am filled with happiness because of the opportunities in this new day. I move beyond past disappointments and pain to claim a new joy in Christ.

I join in community with other disciples of Jesus to sing and rejoice. The melody springs forth as we work and play together giving thanks to God for what is ours in Jesus Christ.

I am thankful for the blessings all around me which are meant to be enjoyed.

"With the judgment you make you will be judged, and the measure you give will be the measure you get." —Matthew 7:2

I am not to set myself up as judge and jury to decide who is worthy or unworthy of God's love. Yet I need to use good judgment when dealing with other people as well as with my own affairs.

I begin to develop sound judgment by calling upon the wisdom God gives as I seek to understand my experiences. As I think about the incidents that reoccur in my life, over time I can see patterns emerge. From these patterns I come to know the steps I will take to create a different future.

It is important to think about my mistakes, and to allow myself to learn from them. In this way I can make the best decisions for myself and the people who will be affected by my choices. Today I empty my mind of cluttering thoughts that keep me from thinking clearly and using sound judgment.

As I deal with people and situations, I call on the wisdom of the Holy Spirit within me to make sound decisions.

There is no fear in love, but perfect love casts out fear.   —1 John 4:18a

There are two kinds of fear. First, there is the fear that warns me of a danger of which I am to be wary. This is a healthy fear which preserves me. The second kind of fear is anxiety that I will fail because I am trying to live up to another's expectations of me or my own sometimes unrealistic expectations.

I need to remember that others will love me because of who I am and not who I think I should be for them. Likewise, I will love others just as they are and for whom God made them to be, so they will not need to live in anxiousness and fear. I know my own anxieties will subside the more I respect and love others.

Today I will tell one or more persons that I appreciate the work they do, how attractively they dress, or how much I enjoy their company. Like me, other people need to hear specifically how they impact my life and are important to me. When people are loved, they can set aside their fear.

I overcome my fear by showing people love and accepting them for who they are.

The fruit of the Spirit is love, joy, peace, patience, kindness, generosity, faithfulness, gentleness, and self-control. . . . If we live by the Spirit, let us also be guided by the Spirit. —Galatians 5:22-23a, 25

Today I slow down and do not feel guilty about "wasting time." I know it is best when I take the time in each day to remember, reflect, and pray. Today I pray that the fruits of the spirit may be seen in the way I live.

Love is expressed as I take time to laugh with my friends. *Peace* is mine when I live each day, one at a time. *Patience* is within me when I wait in hope and expectation, knowing all will be well. *Kindness* is present as I give the benefit of a doubt to another. *Generosity* is known when I give my time to help a co-worker. *Faithfulness* is lived as I continue to struggle with others for consensus and understanding. *Gentleness* is a keystone of my life when I take the effort to walk in another's shoes. *Self-control* is displayed when I make decisions which are helpful to my life and my community.

This day I choose to take time to contemplate the fruits of the Spirit in prayer.

JANUARY 21   LISTENING

Bear one another's burdens, and in this way you will fulfill the law of Christ.   —Galatians 6:2

Today I will listen to others. I will work hard to hear their ideas and not overreact when they voice an opinion that is different from my own.

I may need to set aside my own concerns for some time in order to hear another's cares and burdens. My friends and colleagues need me to listen, not to give my opinion. If they want my opinion, they will ask for it. Even then, I will weigh my reply carefully so that I do not impose my answers on them.

Listening to one who needs to be heard is a gift I give to another. I listen attentively and learn to appreciate each speaker for the unique person he or she is and the thoughts, feelings, and opinions he or she chooses to share with me.

Today I fulfill the law of Christ by listening to another person's worries or cares.

JANUARY 22   LOVE

I pray that you may . . . know the love of Christ that surpasses knowledge, so that you may be filled with all the fullness of God.   —Ephesians 3:18-19

I am learning to view myself with love, compassionately and not abusively. By observing myself interacting with others I gain self-knowledge. It is important that I take the time to know myself and understand why I do the things I do.

In the past I never took the time to develop a sense of my own identity. I was more concerned with what others thought of me than what I thought of myself. I accept the person I am today, even as I continue to grow in knowledge and maturity. I now respect and love myself. In this way I will be able to love others and receive their love.

To grow healthy and whole I will need to establish deep roots grounded in love for God, myself, and others.

From this moment, I embark on a journey in faith to establish myself in love.

❦

JANUARY 23   STRENGTH

I pray that, according to the riches of his glory, he
may grant that you may be strengthened in your
inner being with power through his Spirit.
                                        —*Ephesians 3:16*

Today I am strong and able to live as the
powerful person I am. With God's Spirit
within me, I have the strength to choose bold
new directions for my life. Today I select
activities that reinforce the best of who I am. I
choose only healthy thoughts and emotions,
so that when difficult times arrive I will stand
strong and not be swept away.

I can work on myself knowing that everything will not simply fall into place just
because I understand why I do the things I do.
It will take time to change learned habits and
ways of doing things. It will take time to grow
in strength and power. I will take the time
needed.

I am patient with myself and claim the
strength I have today to live with power
tomorrow.

Therefore confess your sins to one another, and pray for one another, so that you may be healed. The prayer of the righteous is powerful and effective.

—*James 5:16*

I can ask God and other people in my life for help in solving my problems. It is important to tell others what I want and need, as well as how I feel. Healing comes as I am able to recognize where I am broken.

When I knowingly make choices that hurt myself or someone else, I recognize that I have sinned. When I do not hide in shame but admit my sins, I am able to forgive myself and move on. I also ask God and others to forgive me, for that is needful and appropriate.

I am a powerful person, but I also acknowledge that I am not invincible. As I mature in discipleship I can ask others to pray for me as I will pray for others. I no longer have to go it alone. God will give me power to overcome whatever problems come today.

Today I ask for the help and guidance I need to make good decisions.

JANUARY 25   HOLINESS

*You were taught to put away your former way of life
. . . and to be renewed in the spirit of your minds,
and to clothe yourselves with the new self, created
according to the likeness of God in true righteousness
and holiness.*   —Ephesians 4:22-24

I find respect for myself and others as I set
aside the old tattered clothes I used to wear.
The cloth, woven with shame, blame, and
anger, no longer fits me. Today I know which
clothes God has chosen from the closet for me
to wear. God's clothes are woven with righteousness and holiness.

I put on my new self which is kind to me. I
talk and walk respectfully with myself this
day. I take notice of all my attributes that are
holy and right. I am clothed in these peaceful
fabrics which bring tranquillity, not only to
myself but also to others.

**Today I am clothed in the likeness of God
who says I am holy, righteous, and worthy of
respect.**

JANUARY 26   HAPPINESS

Cast all your anxiety on him, because he cares for you.
               —1 Peter 5:7

Today I am content. Because I know that I am cared for by God, I walk through my day with a light step. Incidents that occur today may cause me to feel anxious. These feelings are normal because I am human. But when I feel anxious I don't have to carry the burden alone. I can share the burden with God who cares for me and wants me to be content.

I can choose my own paths to contentment. To be content, I differentiate myself from family members, knowing which emotions are mine and which are theirs. My happiness does not depend on my family's acknowledgment of their problems. Today I know that my parents' problems belong to them and not to me. I am free to live my day without burdening anxiety.

Today I live free, because God cares for me.

JANUARY 27   *ENVY*

Let us not become conceited, competing against one another, envying one another. —*Galatians 5:26*

I appreciate the gifts and talents of my friends and associates. I strive to see the good in others and appreciate their uniqueness. I rejoice that I have such gifted people all around me enriching my days.

In noticing the good things in others I also affirm my own talents and gifts. I am a strong, competent, capable individual. I am friendly and resilient. My unique qualities are appreciated by the people around me.

Both they and I are people of worth, prized for the contributions we each can make. I don't need to earn anything because it is God who gives me worth. Therefore I do not need to compete against other people. They have their purpose and mission in life and I have mine. I value and enjoy the abilities they possess.

I appreciate others for the unique persons God created them to be and also rejoice in my own special talents.

"When the Spirit of truth comes, he will guide you into all the truth." —*John 16:13a*

As a child of the Spirit of truth I refuse to live in darkness again. I will continue to tell the truth always so I do not slip back into old patterns of living which only brought misery. Growing up I learned to communicate in ways that were not direct. It was forbidden in my family to show or tell our true feelings. I learned to leave a trail of clues for others to solve.

I no longer want to play these unproductive games. My emotional life is too important to leave to chance. Today I let my feelings be known in appropriate ways. I am direct in my communication and express how I feel and what I need.

Acknowledging that the Spirit of truth lives within me, I make a conscious decision to communicate directly.

Praise the Lord! Praise the Lord, O my soul! I will praise the Lord as long as I live; I will sing praises to my God all my life long.   —Psalm 146:1-2

I rejoice in who I am today because the power of God is within me. I have opportunities to express God's presence through living fully as the person God designed me to be. I have a choice. I can live dancing gaily or I can stumble wearily along.

Today I will be the special person I am and use my unique abilities. As I dare to be myself, I fully rejoice in the Lord. My life is a shining star which everyone can see, admire, and praise through God. I will be strong, cherish my individuality, and rejoice in the Lord always.

Today I rejoice!

Everything exposed by the light becomes visible, for everything that becomes visible is light. Therefore it says, "Sleeper, awake! Rise from the dead, and Christ will shine on you." —Ephesians 5:13-14

Yesterday in my search for purpose I turned to food, chemicals, drugs, or unhealthy relationships. These dependencies only left me feeling empty and numb. I walked around like a zombie, never feeling truly alive. I refuse to sleepwalk through life.

Today I am awake and free! I declare that I am a child of the Rising Sun and will no longer settle for less than Christ's warmth. I will not depend on things and people to fill my emptiness.

Today I affirm my new alertness which keeps me free from any kind of addiction. My eyes are fully open and my senses are alert, and, with Christ lighting my way, I am ready to move into this new day.

I am free to be awake, alert, alive, and active.

---- 🍂 ----

JANUARY 31   WISDOM

Be careful then how you live, not as unwise people
but as wise, making the most of the time, because the
days are evil.   —*Ephesians 5:15-16*

Today I look at my life with a new understanding of what is important. I act and react
positively to people and my environment. I
take responsibility for the decisions I make,
realizing that living wisely depends on how
clearly I see the realities behind appearances.
How I use my time determines if I will be
content or discontent.

I am wise in that I've decided to be content
and happy now. This means I do not put off
doing the things that are important to me but
I fill my days with choices that are for good
rather than evil.

For years I've wanted to learn to play the
piano, try my hand at painting, or refurbish
furniture. Now I will decide the steps I need
to take to make at least one of my "wants" a
reality.

Today I make the most of my time which is a
gift of God to be used wisely.

FEBRUARY 1   *LOVE*

Those who do not love a brother or sister whom they have seen, cannot love God whom they have not seen.
—*1 John 4:20*b

Jesus loves me, this I know! Because I am loved by God I am able to love myself and others. Sometimes I am tempted not to love others, whom Jesus calls my sisters and brothers, and not to act in loving ways as I live with them. Yet Jesus tells me that loving God and loving others go hand in hand.

I walk through this day with an authority of love. Love radiates from me like the warmth of the sun. Others sense my love and are drawn to me. They, too, want love in their lives. I overcome my isolation and loneliness when I love. I remember that I am chosen to be a radiating center for Christ's divine love.

I love others and act in loving ways because I am grounded in the love of Jesus Christ.

FEBRUARY 2 COMFORT

"In my Father's house there are many dwelling places. If it were not so, would I have told you that I go to prepare a place for you? And if I go and prepare a place for you, I will come again and will take you to myself, so that where I am, there you may be also."
—John 14:2-3

I have called many places home. Childhood homes, dormitory rooms, and apartments—whether luxurious or humble—have been welcoming spaces at the end of long days.

Sometimes, however, I find no rest or comfort—I am restless and anxious regardless of my physical surroundings. I grumble and complain, becoming more and more discontent.

Now I look toward my real home—a home where a place is set at the table just for me and where embracing hugs and words of love welcome me. In prayer I am called to my home in Christ where I find comfort now and always.

Today I remember that my real homeland is in Jesus Christ.

❦

FEBRUARY 3   TRANSFORMATION

Do not be conformed to this world, but be transformed by the renewing of your minds, so that you may discern what is the will of God—what is good and acceptable and perfect.   —Romans 12:2

I am a transforming person! In God's grace and power I can repent (change) and be transformed. With Jesus at my side I can take risks and even make mistakes, confident in a God who loves me and names me acceptable.

Jesus invites me to a life of transformation; to transform my imprisoned self into a free child of God; to transform and relinquish my old plans and be open to God's new possibilities; to transform days of doubt, frustration, and anxiety and be a person who claims and lives God's power.

With God's power in my life I overcome that which keeps me from being the transformed person God intends me to be.

Examine yourselves to see whether you are living in the faith. Test yourselves. Do you not realize that Jesus Christ is in you?—unless, indeed, you fail to meet the test!   *—2 Corinthians 13:5*

"Help! Help! Lord, please save me. I've fallen and I don't know how much longer I can hold on. If you'll just get me down from this cliff I'll do anything."

"Who are you? An angel of the Lord who has come to save me? Great! Then get me down. You have to ask me three questions first?"

"Do I believe in God? Yes, I believe in God!"

"Do I believe in Jesus Christ as my Lord and Savior? Yes, I believe in Jesus Christ as my Lord and Savior!"

"Do I believe that Jesus Christ has the power to save me? Yes! YES! Now please hurry and get me down."

"What? You want me to let go? H-E-L-P!"

From whatever cliff I find myself hanging today, I let go and allow God to work within my life.

FEBRUARY 5   *LOVE*

"You shall love the Lord your God with all your heart, and will all your soul, and with all your mind, and with all your strength . . . [and] your neighbor as yourself."   —Mark 12:30-31a

Jesus tells me to love my neighbor in the same proportion that I love myself. On days when I do not act kindly toward myself, I certainly am equally unkind and unloving toward the people around me. It is true that if I don't love myself I certainly can't love others.

Love is the most therapeutic and healing gift I can give myself and others. I embrace myself with unqualified love and therefore love others. My friends, my spouse, and even my parents may not afford me the love I need, but I realize that the love of God is always in me.

I have love to give others. Love will flow over me and the people around me like a gentle ocean breeze.

Today I let my love flow forth to others.

FEBRUARY 6   FAITH

Keep alert, stand firm in your faith, be courageous,
be strong.   —*1 Corinthians 16:13*

I have choices in life, and I will not act as if
I don't; but, I must make my choices and
claim my rights if I am to have them. Today I
am courageous and strong. I gladly cast the
role of victim aside. I change my pattern of
behavior and act in new ways. I know that I
will survive. I claim the power I have through
faith in Jesus Christ.

I remain alert to people or circumstances
that might want to entrap me. Right now I
live in faith, knowing that God is in charge.

Today I stand firm in my faith, courageous in
the decisions I make and actions I take.

Let all that you do be done in love.
—*1 Corinthians 16:14*

The love my family wanted to give one another was often lost in confusion, fear, and broken promises. Today I set aside those past disappointments and express my love in caring ways by actions and words.

I am learning new ways to be comfortable in my intimacy with others. Sharing deep feelings and thoughts becomes easier as I practice. I am learning to break free from my fears of expressing my deepest feelings to those whom I trust.

How do I tell others I love them? How can I tell others I care? I begin slowly. I don't expect myself to learn it all at once. Expressing love is a gradual process, and I will give myself the time I need.

Today I take a deep breath and acknowledge my fear of sharing my love.

In the morning, while it was still very dark, he [Jesus] got up and went out to a deserted place, and there he prayed.   —Mark 1:35

Today I take the time to pray. I find a quiet space and time to reflect and refocus my journey. I step back from the busyness and clamor of my day to hear what God has to say.

Many times my journey becomes such a struggle that I make myself numb so that I can make it through the day. But I am not content with struggling through my days in numbness.

Today I invite God to sit down with me and give me guidance for the path ahead. I find strength in prayer to live my days as God would have me live them, fully awake and ready to discover the strength within me.

Through prayer I discover a renewed energy for my day.

Therefore, since we are surrounded by so great a cloud of witnesses, let us also lay aside every weight and the sin that clings so closely, and let us run with perseverance the race that is set before us.

—*Hebrews 12:1*

Some sins wrap themselves to me so closely that they are not easily set aside. These are sins which separate me from my intimate relationships with God and the people in my life.

I try to tell myself that the things I do are simply little slips or minor faults, but I do damage to myself when I keep trying to lower the curtain on my pain which comes from not admitting my sin. When I admit my sinfulness, when I admit I am not perfect and not God, I am able to experience and accept the comfort and forgiveness of God.

Today I admit my sins to God who takes my burden. When I let go of the heavy burden I am then freed to run with perseverance the race which is before me.

With my faithful ancestors setting the example, I admit, name, and set aside my sin and run the race with renewed strength and courage.

FEBRUARY 10   GENTLENESS

Let your gentleness be known to everyone. The Lord is near.   *—Philippians 4:5*

Today I am gentle with myself. I look at the expectations I have for myself in a realistic fashion. I know what I am capable of and when I can stretch to expand the realm of possibilities.

I create misery for myself by building unrealistic expectations. When there is no chance of achievement, disatisfaction results. I refuse to build expectations that are a set-up for failure. I also view life realistically for others, expecting only that they are true to who they are.

When I view situations grounded in possibility; when I differentiate between truth and reality; when I work towards possible expectations, I am living gently with myself and my neighbor.

Today I walk gently with myself and my neighbor.

FEBRUARY 11 SELF-ACCEPTANCE

Let no one despise your youth, but set the believers an example in speech and conduct, in love, in faith, in purity.   —*1 Timothy 4:12*

I know whose I am and who I am: a child of God and a person of deep worth. I will let others' criticism pass and feel calm and at ease about who I am.

I hear the views and opinions of others and take what they express as information rather than condemnation. Some of their views may be helpful. Others will not be helpful or accurate, and I set these aside.

In the past I looked to other people's responses when deciding how to act. I used their negative opinions as ammunition against my own sense of self-worth. Today, without shame or anxiety, I weigh what seems helpful. If I choose to change my behavior I do so because I believe I need to and not because I am reacting to anyone else.

I love myself, and my speech and conduct reflect this reality.

FEBRUARY 12   HEALTH

I appeal to you therefore, brothers and sisters, by the mercies of God, to present your bodies as a living sacrifice, holy and acceptable to God, which is your spiritual worship.   —Romans 12:1

I am to present my body, myself, as a person belonging not to this present world but to the coming age. I want my life to encompass a consecrated and holy life-style which gives honor and worship to God.

In this sacrifice my physical body is an intricate part of what I present and who I am. I cannot ignore my body, for it is a vital sign that points to my emotional and spiritual well being. I will not disregard my health but will take good care of my body.

I will not expect myself to change all the old habits at once. Instead, with graciousness, I will make changes one at a time. But, I will begin today!

As I realize that all of who I am is to be worthy of God's calling, I choose to value my body and give it the care God demands.

FEBRUARY 13   MATURITY

When I was a child, I spoke like a child, I thought like a child, I reasoned like a child; when I became an adult, I put an end to childish ways.
—1 Corinthians 13:11

Today I celebrate and rejoice in my adulthood. As I grow older I take satisfaction in my growth in wisdom and insight. I become my own best friend and claim the adult self who changes to behave responsibly with myself and other people.

In the past I hung on to my childish ways. I was resistant to growth because I was afraid of change. As I move into mature adulthood I realize that my old patterns of behaving do not fit with the person I am becoming. Life's lessons have taught me that I can be both giving and receiving in my relationships with other people. I can make careful and respectful choices for myself and the people I love.

I boldly claim my adult status with joy, taking full responsibility for the choices I make and the way I act.

I am an adult child of God who has packed away my childish ways.

—— ❧ ——

FEBRUARY 14   SELF-ACCEPTANCE

I have learned to be content with whatever I have.
—Philippians 4:11b

The apostle Paul often lived in very difficult circumstances, yet he did not spend time nagging and complaining about the way he wished things were. He lived in contentment.

In the past I did not receive enough love, attention, or assurance of my value. Now I have leftover emotional feelings that tell me I need more, and more, and more.

Today I take a moment to center my thoughts on Christ, for when I do this, nothing can disturb or upset me. I need to remember that who I am and what I have are enough.

I choose to turn to the harmony of God's love and be content.

FEBRUARY 15   PRAYER

The end of all things is near; therefore be serious and discipline yourselves for the sake of your prayers.
                                        —*1 Peter 4:7*

Today I take care of my basic emotional and spiritual needs by beginning in prayer. I take the time I need to retreat and give myself the solitude I need.

Sometimes I get so busy rushing from one place to another and one task to another that I lose touch with my prayer relationship with God. With all that is happening in my life, I need time alone with God to experience all of my emotions, thoughts, and deepest longings. I find nourishment when I seek the solitude I need to talk with God in prayer.

Then, when I emerge back into the world, I respond more fully to the rich possibilities for love and service life has to offer. Prayer keeps my life centered so that I can flourish.

I may need to set some tasks aside, but today I take the time to pray.

FEBRUARY 16   CHALLENGES

Those who want to save their life will lose it, and
those who lose their life for my sake, and for the sake
of the gospel, will save it.   —Mark 8:35

What are the prizes in life worth winning?
This is the question that haunts me.

I don't want to rush through life pursuing
one thing after another, only to find in the end
that the only prize worth chasing is the prize
I've managed to lose. I could spend my whole
life collecting the nicest clothes, the smartest
car, or the most notorious name in history and
still lose my own soul.

Jesus asks me even harder questions. What
am I willing to die for, or what in my life
must die so that I can truly live? I may not
always choose the easy ways; in fact, at times
I will need to make hard choices. Some may
be choices for which I even choose to die.

The path I see before me is full of choices.
As a capable adult, I look at the future and
choose those vocations and avocations that
are worthy of my time and calling as a person
of God. I sort out what is important and put
my efforts there.

**Today I choose prizes worthy of my calling as
a disciple of Jesus Christ.**

Why are you cast down, O my soul, and why are you disquieted within me? Hope in God; for I shall again praise him, my help and my God.

—Psalm 43:5

I am a friend to myself, and I stop giving myself disquieting messages. When my inner voice stirs up fear and doubt, I know that these are voices from the past. These critical voices are leftover clutter which no longer belong to who I am, for I am a person of great worth to God.

Perhaps the last obstacle to my spiritual health is facing my sin. The guilt of sin is like a hidden monster under my bed that pops out when I least expect it. Hope in God enables me to recognize and face the guilt and shame of my sin. Only in this way can I begin to quiet the voices that cause my soul to be cast down in despair.

Today as I admit my sin I will substitute old feelings of guilt and shame with positive feelings of peacefulness and contentment.

With hope I face my sin, treat myself with gentle grace, and begin to heal the old wounds.

FEBRUARY 18   BALANCE

I waited patiently for the Lord; he inclined to me and heard my cry. He drew me up from the desolate pit, out of the miry bog, and set my feet upon a rock, making my steps secure. —Psalm 40:1-2

I am stepping out with a greater sense of balance. I don't have to live in the pit of extremes. The world, and my choices in it, are not "all" or "nothing." Instead there are many choices I can make which give balance to my days.

Now I can experience myself in perfect balance. In my health, I am neither overindulgent nor am I neglectful; in my relationships, I am neither clingy nor am I unattached; in my friendships, I am neither overbearing nor am I withdrawn.

Today I have a firm rock to stand on, Jesus Christ, my Lord and Savior. Because of his presence in my life I am learning a new sense of balance in all that I do.

I choose to release all extreme behaviors which keep my life off balance.

— ❦ —

FEBRUARY 19   FEAR

*The Lord is my light and my salvation; whom shall I
fear? The Lord is the stronghold of my life; of whom
shall I be afraid?*   —Psalm 27:1

The power of God lives in all that I see and
do. Because God is with me, taking the lead
on the path, I do not fear. Of course, I will prepare myself as much as possible for whatever
lies ahead, but I also will be still and patient
and know that God will finally use my life
according to God's purpose.

I don't have to live with anxiety attacks or
have a nervous stomach anymore. I know
these physical symptoms are only temporary.
They will subside, and God's peace will
replace them.

I draw on the Lord's strength as I strive to
be who *I am*, instead of who I am *supposed* to
be. I will no longer pay the price for my fears
and false expectations: physical illness, unset-
tledness, compulsiveness, and addiction.
Today I choose the lighted path to happiness,
health, and sanity.

**With the Lord as my light, salvation and
strength, I am unafraid to express myself as
never before.**

"For which of you, intending to build a tower, does not first sit down and estimate the cost, to see whether he has enough to complete it?"   —Luke 14:28

I will accomplish the tasks that I have chosen to undertake. I will survey my work with a new understanding and look at how I can put the large job into manageable, do-able components. In this way I will not be overwhelmed by the enormity of the big picture. Neither will I allow myself to be stuck in the small details of the task, but I will do what needs to be accomplished and move on.

I find balance in the work I do. My projects do not define who I am or my worth to God. Therefore, as I undertake each assignment I take on, I learn from both my successes and my failures. I seek assistance as I need it and find guidance and insight from my colleagues and associates.

I no longer expect perfection in everything I do. Instead, I do the best I can in each instance, with the constraints the situation places upon the work.

Today I am a builder who makes a workable, realistic plan of action and works one step at a time toward completion.

"Which of these three, do you think, was a neighbor to the man who fell into the hands of the robbers?" He said, "The one who showed him mercy." Jesus said unto him, "Go and do likewise." —Luke 10:36-37

I can help other people and also take care of my own needs. I can show other people mercy with acts of kindness and care without becoming exhausted or burned out. When I nurture and support my friends or a stranger, I do so without giving away so much of myself that I jeopardize my own health.

If I fail to care for my own spiritual, emotional, and bodily needs, I am of no help to anyone. Today I seek support and nourishment from my friends and especially from God whose ready arm supplies my needs.

As I take time to assure that my own needs are being met in healthy ways, I give of my time and energy and lend a helping hand to my neighbor.

Teach me your way, O Lord, and lead me on a level path.   —*Psalm 27:11*a

Today I look at unspoken rules that control my actions. I know I continue to live by rules that are no longer congruent with who I am.

I once drew a map, with highways and paths, which seemed accurate in directing my journey. This map proved to be full of dead ends and detours. Now I must crumple up this map and begin again to write new directions to guide my choices. On this map I find new, uncharted routes which work.

As I realign my guideposts, I seek new people who accept me for who I am and who nurture me in the ways of discipleship. I look for opportunities in work and play that enhance and use the gifts God places within me.

As a child of God on the path, I re-evaluate the guideposts to make them relevant to who I am now.

Fathers, do not provoke your children, or they may lose heart. —Colossians 3:21

As a parent, I have the opportunity to participate in my children's emerging self-discovery. Today I look at my skills of parenting and am aware of how I act and react. My aim is to model skills that will help my children lead happy, productive lives. I have learned from the actions of my parents, and now I listen for a loving parental voice as I speak to my children.

I now have the opportunity to model self-acceptance, firmness, and balance to my children. I have a warm heart which allows me to hug and kiss my children and let them know how greatly I love and care for them. I treat them in ways that allow them to be the wonderful persons they are.

My children are magnificent children of God. I cherish and respect them so they will possess a strong heart for the road ahead.

I honor and respect the persons my children are becoming.

—— ❦ ——

FEBRUARY 24   PRAYER

And after he had dismissed the crowds, he went up the mountain by himself to pray. When evening came, he was there alone.   —Matthew 14:23

Taking time in my rigorous daily schedule to pray is like a breath of fresh air. I know that by allowing time to pray, I make room so God can act more fully in my life.

I am no longer afraid of facing my inner self in prayer. It is important to take a step back from the problems of home or work and look at them from a reflective, prayerful perspective. It is up to me to take the time I need to be alone in prayer. I will protect this time and not let other activities spill over into these precious moments spent between myself and God.

Today I make specific plans to pray, and I follow through. I write the appointment on my calendar and take it seriously. I am motivated to finish my other tasks so I can enjoy this time of prayer.

I learn to plan my time so I can enjoy reflection, meditation, and prayer.

Finally, beloved, whatever is true, whatever is honorable, whatever is just, whatever is pure, whatever is pleasing, whatever is commendable, if there is any excellence and if there is anything worthy of praise, think about these things.　　—Philippians 4:8

I need special moments in my life. It's the smile when I'm feeling down or the simple compliment that puts a bounce in my step and joy in my day.

I enjoy sharing laughter with friends and a cup of coffee and conversation with a colleague. These moments are filled with meaning that I do not want to miss. On some days, the special moments are what keep me going when I'd rather quit.

I capture and enjoy moments that are full and abundant. I pay attention and participate in good times with good people. I am learning to enjoy the lovely small gestures and remarks that make the days bright. Life is full of wonder and delight when I take time to notice and join in.

As I think on truth, justice, honor, purity, pleasure, and excellence, I give praise to God!

🍒

FEBRUARY 26   SEXUALITY

There is no longer Jew or Greek, there is no longer slave or free, there is no longer male or female; for all of you are one in Christ Jesus. —Galatians 3:28

Our culture has sent mixed messages about what divides me from other people. The biblical writer reinforces that I am one with other people in Christ, and therefore I share spiritual kinship with them. When I live my relationships with others in these open ways, I am fulfilling God's promise.

As I grow to know myself, I've come to accept and appreciate the wonders of all the characteristics within me, both masculine and feminine. Today I affirm who I am, male or female, and reject the distorted views of the past. I affirm my sexuality and the unique beauty it holds. I celebrate the sexual person that's a part of who I am as a whole person of God. In Christ I am free to share in spiritual kinship with all people as an equal in Christ Jesus.

Today I do away with artificial barriers and share with others a mutual spiritual life in Christ.

FEBRUARY 27   ACCEPTANCE

"Why do you see the speck in your neighbor's eye, but do not notice the log in your own eye?" —Luke 6:41

Today I accept others as well as myself. I recognize that I and others will make mistakes, and I am gentle and forgiving.

I am learning to be gracious toward others and accept the job that they do as an offering of their best ability in each moment. In this way I am learning to be gracious and less judgmental toward myself. I can accept that I will do the best I can, for the person I am, in each moment.

I cast away the critical, demanding self which limits my potential and creates loneliness. I admit my weaknesses without feeling ashamed. I accept that others have answers and solutions that I do not have from my own scope of experience.

I give God thanks as I appreciate and accept others.

---❦---

FEBRUARY 28   MATERIALISM

"Therefore I tell you, do not worry about your life, what you will eat, or about your body, what you will wear. For life is more than food, and the body more than clothing."   —Luke 12:22-23

I am no longer weighed down by the need for many material things. When I search outside myself for possessions to fill the void, I am left feeling empty and barren. My compulsive buying is a symptom of what I really search for: peace of mind and contentment in life. Things do not have the power to meet these needs.

Now, as I center on Jesus Christ and a life of discipleship, I focus my energy on my desire to serve God, and I therefore feel good about myself emotionally, physically, mentally, and spiritually. When I align myself with God and God's power, my days are put to good use.

I am freed from compulsive buying for instant gratification which gives peace for only a brief moment. To find happiness I do not need to reach outside myself but only to the Holy Spirit who dwells within.

I seek God's place in my life first.

"But a Samaritan while traveling came near him; and when he saw him, he was moved with pity. He went to him and bandaged his wounds, having poured oil and wine on them. Then he put him on his own animal, brought him to an inn, and took care of him."   —Luke 10:33-34

When needed, I can be responsible for my relative, friend, or neighbor and help them out of my own strength. Being responsible for other persons simply means that I do the best I can for them. I respect them as persons of dignity who, in times of need, are worthy of my help.

I live my responsibility for my neighbor and friend without feeling a need to control them or their lives. Unhealthy responsibility for others results in manipulative, controlling behavior. Being controlling of others means I blame myself when they fail. I will not delude myself into believing I can control the outcome of their lives. This understanding frees me to love and give aid to my friend in helpful ways.

I show care for my friends, relatives, and neighbors in ways that are healing and respectful of myself and them.

MARCH 2 ATTITUDE

I will bless the Lord at all times; his praise continually be in my mouth. —Psalm 34:1

The thoughts that produce what I say aloud are a reflection of what I believe. When I spend my energy thinking and talking in positive ways, my life manifests itself in that reality. When I spend time praising God and giving thanks for the blessings of this day, I am attuned to the positive within me. I act in self-assured, healthy ways as I experience the comfort and security of God in my life.

Today I take time to feed healthy messages to myself, thereby affecting the words that come from my lips. This improves the mental image I have of myself and instills positive and powerful determination in my behavior now and in the future.

I take time to think about God who cares for me and to give praise to God for the created world.

MARCH 3   CHANGE

Prove me, O Lord, and try me; test my heart and mind. For your steadfast love is before my eyes, and I walk in faithfulness to you.   —Psalm 26:2-3

I refuse to deceive myself any longer by avoiding the confrontation which keeps me stuck and unable to move on. When I refuse to face what needs to be changed, I stifle my own growth and development.

In the past I avoided facing conflict and confrontation at any price. It was better to live in the agony of the present circumstances— where I knew what to expect and could act accordingly—than to forge forward into the unknown. I was willing to live life in a flat, colorless malaise rather than trust God and risk the unknown possibilities of the future.

Today I stop living in numbing ways. I explore uncharted territories as I examine my relationships at home and at work. I make choices which release me to live in faithfulness to the person God calls me to be.

I trust God to help me encounter and change that which keeps me stuck in old patterns.

—— ❧ ——

MARCH 4   HOPE

*They confronted me in the day of my calamity; but
the Lord was my support.*   —Psalm 18:18

I am encouraged and I share this encouragement with others. In the past I was unable to
share this optimistic understanding of life
because I barely believed it myself. I was troubled by fear of rejection and criticism. Today I
accept myself and other people.

When I am discouraged I will strive to
remain open and remember how God has
worked through my life in times past. I draw
hope in knowing that I have made it through
rougher times than these and I will make it
through this time as well.

**I am thankful that God encourages me and
challenges me to "keep on keeping on."**

MARCH 5   STRENGTH

Blessed are the poor in spirit, for theirs is the kingdom of heaven.   —*Matthew 5:3*

I know I need God to strengthen me. That is what being "poor in spirit" means.

Sometimes I try to mend the pieces of my life that have come apart by gluing them back together as I might try to tape and glue a dismantled picture frame. But, like the poorly repaired frame that gives way and falls to the floor with a bang, these temporary remedies fail, and my "frame" once again bends under the pressure, crumbles, and comes crashing down. Then I realize that, with God, I have the strength to make a lasting repair.

I know that God will give me the strength I need to make lifelong repairs.

—— 🍂 ——

MARCH 6   FORGIVENESS

Blessed are those who mourn, for they will be comforted.
                                    —Matthew 5:4

I have a sense of failure, guilt, and mourning when I fear that others have seen my worst side—not the shiny best I want them to see. Yet when I bring myself before the cross of Jesus, all of who I am is exposed. It can be terrifying indeed to face myself as I am!

Today I will mourn, see myself as I truly am, and seek pardon. I will make amends—with myself, as well as with others and with God. Accepting Christ's assuring love and forgiveness I will begin again, forgiven and comforted. I will do the best I can for who I am in each moment I live.

I do not despair, for God's assuring love embraces me in divine arms and releases me as forgiven.

Blessed are the meek, for they will inherit the earth.
—*Matthew 5:5*

To become meek, I must give my life to Jesus Christ and allow him to become the center of my life.

As a child, I played with dominoes, setting them up on end, side by side. This game would continue until one piece tipped over and caused all the others to tumble down.

Like that game of dominoes, I once tried to build a life I could control. Carefully, I made decisions and choices, based upon the foundation of my own endeavors. But ultimately they tumbled down.

Today I ask Jesus to help me release my tight grip of control.

Today I look for ways and opportunities to be meek, to let go, and to allow Jesus to lead me in God's way.

MARCH 8   WHOLENESS

Blessed are those who hunger and thirst for right-
eousness, for they will be filled.   —Matthew 5:6

I feel an urgent need as I search for God, for I know there is satisfaction and stability in doing God's will. Today I accept that my need is the hunger inside me—the small child within who never receives enough. As I accept my hunger, I awaken to discover ways to fill that emptiness. Each situation and person I meet offers an opportunity to allow Christ to fill me with new ways of being.

I do not want to deprive myself in life. Instead, my appetite is strong. With Jesus beside me, my voice speaks boldly, and I choose to live life to its fullest. I am positive and energetic, because I know that Jesus wants to fill me with good things to satisfy my need and my hunger.

Today I admit my need so that it can be filled.

—— ❦ ——

MARCH 9   MERCY

Blessed are the merciful, for they will receive mercy.
—*Matthew 5:7*

Holier-than-thou attitudes have no place in my life. I give mercy freely because I know that I have freely received mercy from God.

I not only have mercy for others, but I also ask God to help me have mercy for myself. At times I become impatient. I want to rid myself of all my faults immediately. But, with God's help, I can piece together my life, as if I were sewing a patchwork quilt. A quilt-maker does not discard odd shapes but fits them into place to create a final artistic design.

With love and patience, I am learning to accept and appreciate my odd shapes and to piece them together in new ways. A work of art is in the making.

Today I give and receive mercy when I pick up someone who falls, when I offer my hand to someone who stumbles, and when I weep with someone who hurts.

Blessed are the pure in heart, for they will see God.
—*Matthew 5:8*

Children are pure in heart; they look at their world with clear eyes, open arms, and a trusting attitude. They see the world with wonder and simple honesty. They react spontaneously to the events of their day; what they feel is who they are.

When I watch children playing, I realize how complex I've made my own life. I carry old baggage from the past as I walk into the future of today. I drag through my day with clouded eyes. I am not in touch with my feelings.

Children teach us lessons of wonder and trust. They instinctively trust those who care for them. I have a Savior who cares for me and has everything under control. I will trust my Savior once again.

I pray to have the heart of a child, to be pure in heart.

MARCH 11   PEACE

Blessed are the peacemakers, for they will be called
children of God.   —*Matthew 5:9*

In a harsh world torn by fear, anger, and vio-
lence, I am called by Jesus to be a person of
peace. I will create an environment of peace
around me. I will live in ways that maintain
harmony with myself, with others, and with
God.

I live and work with people who do not
carry this understanding of amity. When I
encounter them, it is easy to become caught
up in their tugging and pulling, their artificial
chaos.

But today I will remain calm and composed.
I will live my life in ways that reflect the
peace of mind and soul that is within me.
This unshakeable peace frames my life. Following the example of Jesus, I will be a maker
of peace.

Today I live within the peace that Jesus gives.

Blessed are those who are persecuted for righteousness' sake, for theirs is the kingdom of heaven.
—*Matthew 5:10*

To Matthew, righteousness meant doing what God requires.

Sometimes when I do what I believe God asks me to do, people criticize me. When this happened in the past, I began to doubt myself, thinking that perhaps there was something wrong with me. I grew silent in the face of my persecutors and sulked as I crept away.

Those are old patterns of behavior. Today I calmly and gracefully handle all that confronts me. I allow the power given by Jesus to fill my consciousness. Harmony and balance are restored, and an overall vision of well-being is growing in my life.

I am peaceful and strong before people who persecute me.

MARCH 13   STRENGTH

You are the salt of the earth; but if salt has lost its taste, how can its saltiness be restored?

—Matthew 5:13a

When I accept Jesus' call to be the salt of the earth, I give flavor to the world around me. I dance upon this earth and conserve God's goodness in the events and people I encounter.

To preserve my own saltiness, I will take care that I do not become "burned out." I will find the nourishment and support I need in those I trust. I do an injustice to others, as well as to myself, when I do not take care of myself.

Today I resolve to attend to my own needs. I will find nurture and support in my friends and in Jesus Christ. In this way, I will have the endurance required to live as the salt of the earth.

In Jesus Christ, I have the strength to endure and to dance through whatever comes my way today.

MARCH 14   DISCIPLESHIP

You are the light of the world. A city built on a hill cannot be hid.   —Matthew 5:14

To be known as a disciple of Jesus, I will live out the qualities of a disciple. A disciple's light emanates from God, and today I will reflect this light.

A crystal prism hanging in the sunlight flashes sparkling rays of rainbow colors in many directions. People are drawn to its light because of the contrast to the stark gray world in which it shimmers. Do I dare to be such a light in the world? Do I dare to stand up and be the gifted person I was created to be?

There are days when I simply want to hide, so as not to be hurt. It is much easier and less costly to simply blend in. But today I will be a light. I am optimistic about the experiences and people that Jesus will bring into my life.

I am a candle for Jesus Christ today—at home, or at the office, or at the store, or in the car.

Unless your righteousness exceeds that of the scribes and the Pharisees, you will never enter the kingdom of heaven.   *—Matthew 5:20*

Jesus is not telling me that I must be perfect to be worthy to enter God's home. Rather, he is telling me to live beyond the rules, to live according to what is right and true in God's sight.

When I speak what I know to be right and true, I am filled with God's power. I am keenly aware of my commitment to speak and live the truth, and I will do so with compassion and kindness toward others and myself.

With the help of the Holy Spirit, I speak, feel, and live in truthful, righteous ways.

---

*But I say to you that if you are angry with a brother
or sister, you will be liable to judgment.*
>   *—Matthew 5:22a*

Today I will make healthy, rational decisions about how to deal with my anger. I will
not let anger rule my life.

At one time I thought that if I cut myself
off from my rage, it would go away. But today
I know the high cost of cutting myself off
from my emotions. When I deny my feelings, I
bring judgment upon myself in the form of
headaches, backaches, and stomachaches.

Today is the day I will stop letting my anger
run my life and relationships. I will work on
the skills needed to resolve my anger. I will
not direct my anger unjustly at my children,
my partner, or my colleagues. Instead, I will
turn to God and others for the assistance I
need in rechanneling my feelings.

**Whether through prayer and fasting, journal-
ing, talking with a friend, or counseling, I
search out ways to work through my anger.**

Leave your gift there before the altar and go; first be reconciled to your brother or sister. —Matthew 5:24a

I am no longer afraid of being angry. My anger tells me there is something discordant in my relationship with my brother or sister.

In the past I used much energy in an attempt to repress anger, because I was afraid of alienating people and destroying relationships. I made myself numb in the process. I accumulated little bits of anger in my "slush pot" until it boiled and turned to rage—rage that I was fearful to express.

Now I am able to listen to my anger and hear how I need to change. I can make the decision to express my anger openly, honestly, and appropriately. Today I will talk with the person with whom I am angry. I do not want this relationship to die because of unexpressed anger.

With Jesus' help, I clear the air with honesty.

※

MARCH 18   *HONESTY*

*And if your right hand causes you to sin, cut it off
and throw it away.*
                              —*Matthew 5:30a*

Being honest in personal relationships is
part of living as a disciple of Jesus Christ. As I
deal with those I love, I will express my
desires directly, without using manipulative
behavior—setting myself up for sympathy by
placing guilt or playing victim. I know that
these actions only breed resentment.

Today I will cultivate honesty through my
actions and words. I am ready to "cut off and
throw away" coercive manipulation as a strategy. I will nurture my relationships with people I love by being intentionally faithful to my
promises. In this way, I can stand in an honest
relationship with the most honest one, Jesus
Christ, my Lord.

**Today I live in honesty by keeping the sacred
commitments I have made with the people I
love.**

---●---

MARCH 19   DECISIONS

*Let your word be "Yes, Yes" or "No, No"; anything
more than this comes from the evil one.*
—*Matthew 5:37a*

I will simplify my thinking today. Sometimes my thoughts become muddled as I am
caught up in crosscurrents of confusion.
Today I will stop and take time to look at the
Yeses and Nos of my decisions. I will resist
becoming overwhelmed in a complicated
home or work situation by carefully consider-
ing the pros and cons.

When it is time for a decision, I will be
aligned with the Holy Spirit's work within
me, and I will find clarity. I will let Jesus
Christ guide my Yes and my No.

**The order of Christ is in my life, firmly estab-
lished in simplicity.**

MARCH 20   SURRENDER

But I say to you, Do not resist an evildoer.
—Matthew 5:39a

I will live by a different standard for righting wrongs. Jesus says I am to resist the desire to get even. This teaching calls for great confidence in God.

My urge to get even continues to deplete my energies by causing me to concentrate on matters I cannot change. Today I surrender the hurt I feel to Jesus for resolution. I trust him to help me let go of circumstances I cannot control and alleviate the stress that stems from my compulsive reactions to others' decisions.

Today I surrender my desires for revenge to Jesus and begin again, renewed and fresh.

—— ❦ ——

MARCH 21   RELATIONSHIPS

But I say to you, Love your enemies and pray for those who persecute you.   —Matthew 5:44

Love your enemies! Just the thought of it causes me to cringe. I will need strength from Jesus to do what is expected.

Today I recognize that those I label enemies at work or at church are only frail people, with shortcomings and faults like my own. They do the best they can, as I do the best I can. This does not mean that I should put my life in their hands or let them make decisions for me. But it does mean that I can stop the vicious cycle of hate.

It is hard to act in loving ways toward those I feel are not on my side. Thank God I have the Holy Spirit to help me.

Today I experience new freedom in Christ as I act in loving ways.

MARCH 22 SELF-ACCEPTANCE

Beware of practicing your piety before others in order to be seen by them. —Matthew 6:1a

In the eyes of Jesus, everyone is on top. Today my sense of self is secure and I have no doubt about my worth.

The source of my approval does not reside in other people. I no longer need to "audition" for others, hoping they will affirm my worth. When I pretend to be someone I'm not, I alienate myself from others and from God.

When I'm feeling good about who I am, I don't need to put on airs. I simply accept myself and expect others to do the same. I am in the process of building a firm foundation of self-acceptance in Jesus Christ.

Though self-doubt may ooze into my consciousness, I know that the foundation of acceptance in Jesus Christ is sure.

When you give alms, do not let your left hand know what your right hand is doing. —Matthew 6:3

I am keenly aware of my desire to give. Jesus tells me that it is important for me to want to give. The way I share and the attitude I have when I give to others are also important.

In the past I was caught up in what others might think, so my gift needed to be perfect. I also looked for the correct response to my generosity from the person who received the gift.

This year my giving will be different. I will not choose my gifts, or their recipients, to impress. Instead I give in a way that expresses my love to those who are special. And as I give to my church, to charities, and to my family, I demonstrate my love.

I practice acts of kindness that acknowledge God's presence through Jesus Christ.

MARCH 24   SELF-ACCEPTANCE

And whenever you pray, do not be like the hypocrites.
—Matthew 6:5a

Today I am confident of myself, unconcerned about what other people think of me. If I choose to act in a certain way, it is to please myself and God, and no one else.

Today I recognize, without shame or anxiety, that others' opinions do not control my feelings or behavior. If I feel bound by what other people think or say or do, I stop to decide what Jesus wants for my life.

I accept myself, knowing that the Holy Spirit is working within me.

MARCH 25   SELF-ACCEPTANCE

Whenever you pray, go into your room and shut the door and pray to your Father.   —Matthew 6:6a

I no longer feel a desperate need for people's approval. Today I relate to my friends and colleagues as a person with a deep conviction of self-worth. With the strength of my integrity, I no longer need to display my personal piety before others.

Some parts of my relationship with God are private, not meant to be shared with others. I cherish the times I spend alone with God in prayer. In those moments, I stand by myself with God, loved and accepted.

I envision myself enfolded in the love of the One who names me acceptable—Jesus Christ, my Lord.

———— ❧ ————

MARCH 26   PRAYER

*For your Father knows what you need before you ask
him. Pray then in this way.*   —*Matthew* 6:8b-9a

I have heard the warning: "Be careful what
you pray for, because you will get it." Looking
back through my life, I see that this is true.

Today I'm very careful about what I pray
for. I pray less for specifics and more for wisdom. When I ask God questions, I listen for
God's answers—not mine. I ask for God's
guidance for living faithfully—living each day
as best I can.

Today I ask the Lord to teach me to pray.

—— ❧ ——

MARCH 27 REVERENCE

Our Father in heaven, hallowed be your name.
—Matthew 6:9b

What can I do during the day that will hallow and respect God's name? What of myself can I lift up as an offering to a holy God?

I hallow God's name when I see the positive in myself and in each person I meet; when I care for my body with adequate rest, appropriate food, and sufficient exercise; when I make choices that are loving and that respect the people with whom I live and work.

I am blessed with a holy God who names me acceptable and loved. As I move through this day, I can hallow God's name by affirming the goodness in myself and in other people.

Today I hallow God's name and, therefore, honor this day.

Your kingdom come. Your will be done, on earth as it is in heaven.   —*Matthew 6:10*

Today I put my ego aside and let the Holy Spirit work freely through me.

At times when incidents in my life left me discouraged and disappointed, I thought that God had deserted me. Today I recall that God is always with me. Whatever I need, whether it be big or small, I can turn to God for help.

I know there is direction for me. I pray and listen and allow God's will to be done.

Today I allow Jesus to work in my life to the fullest.

---- ❦ ----

MARCH 29   NEEDS

Give us this day our daily bread.   —*Matthew 6:11*

Sometimes I wonder if I will have enough faith, courage, strength, or self-esteem to make it through the difficult times in my life. But I am reassured that God will give me what I need, when I need it. Just as a mother gives her child the money to buy bread when she sends the child to the store, and not before, so also God provides for me.

God gives me bread to fully live my days, not to just muddle through. God gives me bread to live—not only for today, but for each tomorrow—one day at a time. Today I thank God for meeting my needs.

Each day I seek God's bread for my life.

MARCH 30   FORGIVENESS

And forgive us our debts, as we also have forgiven our debtors. —*Matthew 6:12*

To give my heart only to have it rejected is one of life's greatest sorrows. But I am comforted and strengthened by the example of Jesus. Jesus did not give up in the face of repeated rejection. Instead, he forgave us and came to offer his love again. And he keeps coming, because he is the faithful One who has bound himself to his people.

Today I forgive those who hurt me because they are not able to give me the love and acceptance I seek.

MARCH 31   TRIALS

And do not bring us to the time of trial, but rescue us from the evil one.   —Matthew 6:13

During times of hard testing, I resist the temptation to compromise my faith in Jesus Christ. I choose not to participate in an activity I know to be wrong but to express what I know to be right. I live by the Christian standards I know are right.

As I fully claim the power of the Holy Spirit, I speak up and state my position. I can say either yes or no to those who ask me to participate. And I expect my decisions to be respected, just as I respect the decisions of others.

With the help of Jesus, I resist temptation.

APRIL 1   FORGIVENESS

For if you forgive others their trespasses, your heavenly Father will also forgive you.   —Matthew 6:14

God's forgiveness is a word of grace. Often I get so preoccupied with the hustle and bustle of each day that I lose sight of God's presence in my life. But just when I stumble and begin to panic because I feel lost, God reaches out in grace to touch my life—just as a parent gives a reassuring touch to a troubled child who has lost sight of Mom or Dad in a busy crowd.

Regardless of how far I may stray, God is always there to enfold me in grace. Because I am forgiven, I am able to forgive others; and because I forgive others, God also forgives me. Today I thank God for the gift of forgiveness.

I am thankful for God's forgiving grace in my life, for God's grace touches before I reach, answers before I ask, and comes before I call.

But when you fast, put oil on your head and wash your face, so that your fasting may be seen not by others but by your Father.   —Matthew 6:17-18

Jesus knew the importance of building a strong spiritual life. It is good to reserve parts of my life and experiences just for God and myself. I do not need to parade my acts of self-denial in front of others so that they will admire me. Some things must be done apart from others.

I need relationships, but I do not define myself by the people who surround me or by the roles I play. I will keep these special times between God and myself private so that I may see God through my own experience rather than filtered through others' reactions.

Because my personal relationship with Jesus is important, I keep the sacred sacred.

APRIL 3   CHOICES

Where your treasure is, there your heart will be also.
—Matthew 6:21

Jesus' words can be applied to the things I depend on for my personal identity. As I choose my treasure, I determine those things that will be in the center of my life.

My relationships with God, others, and myself are the investments in which I regularly deposit time, energy, and new awareness. I withdraw from old patterns that lead me away from that which I regard as important. My treasure is my love for Jesus Christ and for the people God has placed in my life. This is where my heart is.

I invest my energy, my time, and my love in Jesus Christ, who is at the center of my treasure chest.

——— ❧ ———

APRIL 4   GUIDANCE

If your eye is healthy, your whole body will be full of light.   —*Matthew* 6:22b

What I see through my attitudes can give me satisfaction and hope or lead me to unhappiness and defeat. If my eye is healthy, my life is one of light.

Today I am glad to be alive. I give thanks to God for my life, knowing that with each new challenge I grow in faith. Jesus has given me a mission in life. As I seek to fulfill my purpose and live a life of light, I know that Jesus continues to guide me.

I take a few quiet moments to look ahead, so that I may see where Jesus is guiding me.

APRIL 5   CHOICES

No one can serve two masters.   —*Matthew 6:24*

I am discovering new ways to make healthy choices. I can choose God's ways, or I can choose paths that lead me away from God. I know that when I try to facilitate both, I become divided within and despise myself.

Today I have the wisdom to know that I must think before I act. I can avoid impulsive behavior. This is not being indecisive; it is being a disciplined disciple.

If I find myself divided as to what choice to make, I take time to pray and listen to God. I do not react to what other people may think is right for my life. I act in ways that serve a risen Savior.

I consider my choices seriously today.

APRIL 6   WORRY

And can any of you by worrying add a single hour to your span of life?   —Matthew 6:27

Today I live boldly without worrying. I experiment with chances I never have taken before.

I refuse to live such a staid and sensible life day after day! I do not become bogged down in apprehension and anxiety about what "could" happen. I refuse to go through life being one of those people who never try to achieve a new height for fear of falling.

After living boldly today I still may have real problems, but I will have fewer imagined ones! I will savor this day that the Lord has made! I will rejoice and be glad!

I take risks and even make mistakes, having confidence in a God who loves me and calls me acceptable.

APRIL 7   WORRY

So do not worry about tomorrow, for tomorrow will bring worries of its own. Today's trouble is enough for today.   —Matthew 6:34

After living a life so carefully measured and controlled by worry, I claim my new freedom in Jesus Christ! I will cross more bridges, climb more mountains, and eat more chocolate cake and less asparagus (or more asparagus and less chocolate cake).

Today I put all my "but what ifs" aside and take more chances. I do not live days or weeks ahead, but I experience this day fully. I relax, consider what is truly important to me, and invest my energy there.

Because of Christ's love, I embrace life today without worry.

How can you say to your neighbor, Let me take the speck out of your eye, while the log is in your own eye?
—Matthew 7:4

Let me be gentle today. Let me cast aside the part of myself that judges others and myself unworthy. Let me relax and become less brittle, less rigid.

I am tender toward myself and toward others. I experience this day without demanding perfection from myself or from others. When I am hard on myself, the harshness spills over into my relationships. Today I walk gently, assured of who I am.

Today I am gentle with others and show them that they are wanted, needed, and accepted.

APRIL 9   DISCERNMENT

Do not throw your pearls before swine.
—Matthew 7:6b

Although I would like to share my faith freely with all people, I cannot. Some people would not understand and would label me "one of those." And there are some people who are extremely difficult—people whom only God can handle.

As I deal with people today, with God's help, I communicate in straightforward, loving ways—without sarcasm or resentment. I am tactful with others, expressing what I want to say with understanding and patience.

I remember that I can do only what is humanly possible. My inner strength, fed by the Holy Spirit, leads me to discriminate in my encounters so that I can have healthy relationships.

Today I am discerning as I share my personal faith with others.

─── ❦ ───

APRIL 10   DISCERNMENT

Ask, and it will be given you; search, and you will find.
                                    —*Matthew 7:7a*

I am asking. I am searching. I am knocking. I recognize that mere survival is not enough. God wants me to be nurtured and flourish. So I am asking God for wisdom. I am searching for knowledge. I am knocking for discernment.

But first, I must admit what I need. I must be willing to lay myself open and know who I am in order to know and name my needs. Then I must decide that I want those needs to be met.

Today I focus energy on knowing myself. I observe myself in interaction with others. In this way, I develop a sense of who I am and what I truly need.

Today I seek and knock on the door of insight and love.

Is there anyone among you who, if your child asks for bread, will give a stone? —Matthew 7:9

It would be ridiculous to give my children a rock if they asked for a slice of bread. Yet that is exactly what can happen if I do not listen to what my children are telling me.

I learned from my own parents ways of interacting with children, ways that guide my parenting today. Some ways I repeat; others I put aside as unhelpful.

Today I love my children by caring enough to set limits. I discipline with respect. I take opportunities to model firmness, acceptance, and self-esteem. I teach the skills necessary for them to live healthy, productive lives. And, if I need help in parenting, I seek guidance.

I know that I have important gifts to give my children as I participate in their gradual self-discovery.

How much more will your Father in heaven give good things to those who ask him! —Matthew 7:11b

The harsh winter winds are passing, and I have a new and abiding warmth in my soul. In this warmth of Jesus Christ, I am learning how to receive. It is important to teach myself how to be a gracious receiver and accept the good that Jesus has given me.

Today I challenge all that I have been taught about receiving. A gift is not a reward for something I have done. The Lord has pleasure in simply giving, and I can enjoy the gift and therefore the giver. I am thankful for God's gifts.

I am growing in Christ when I give myself permission to experience the pleasure of being a joyful receiver.

I thank God for the good things I enjoy.

In everything do to others as you would have them do to you.   —*Matthew 7:12a*

Jesus gives this guideline for living positively, with mercy and grace. Knowing how much I need mercy, I can extend mercy to others. Knowing how much I need compassion, I can extend compassion to others. Knowing how much I need love, I can extend love to others.

When I know myself and am aware of my own needs, shortcomings, and sins, I am not as quick to judge others, and I have more patience with my own faults.

Today I am gentle in my actions, because I want others to act more gently with me. With Jesus by my side I accept responsibility for the way I treat others.

I treat others as I would have them treat me— with kindness, gentleness, and mercy.

The gate is narrow and the road is hard that leads to life, and there are few who find it. —Matthew 7:14

Jesus calls me to make a decision. I write my life story by the decisions I make. Yet some major decisions will determine the many smaller ones that follow. Any decision, any gate, has its consequences.

The road in life that God has set before me is never easy, and I cannot make the trip alone. I need the Holy Spirit, who sustains and guides me. I also need people who share my down times as well as my up times; and I do the same for them.

Today I take time to meditate, to slow down, and to connect with the Holy Spirit working within me. I use this time to contemplate my friendships and my direction in life.

Guided by Christ, I take the narrow gate and seek companions along the way to walk with me.

APRIL 15 DISCERNMENT

Beware of false prophets, who come to you in sheep's clothing. . . . Thus you will know them by their fruits.
—*Matthew 7:15a, 20*

I ask for God's guidance in evaluating what I see, what I feel, and what I sense. If a circumstance or relationship does not feel right to me, I name it. I do not depend upon what other people tell me if it does not coincide with perceptions I know to be true.

In the past I sometimes disregarded my own warning signals. I entered situations I knew were dangerous and rushed into relationships I knew were not good for me. With God's help, today I am learning to see people and situations for who and what they are—not for what I wish them to be.

I am undeniably connected to God, who helps me examine the situations and people I encounter.

*On that day many will say to me, "Lord, Lord, did
we not prophesy in your name?"*   —Matthew 7:22a

Lord, am I one of those people who think
they are doing your will but are not? Today
I cultivate self-observation and learn to be
truthful.

I am developing a high degree of honesty as
I strive to live each day by what I believe.
What I say and do will be synonymous. I will
be honest with others, with myself, and with
God.

Constant denial has caused me hurt and
disappointment in the past. Today I will face
facts and take responsibility for my choices
and actions. In this way I can live my day
truthfully before God.

**I live in honesty to honor my Lord, Jesus
Christ, and myself.**

Everyone then who hears these words of mine and acts on them will be like a wise man who built his house on a rock.   —Matthew 7:24

Wet sand has such malleability that it can be shaped and reshaped again and again. Sand is good for certain purposes. But rock is different. A large rock remains in the same position year after year. For the purpose of building a house, Jesus says that I should use rock.

As a hearer of the lessons of Jesus and a doer of Jesus' ways, I need to remember the foundation of my life and faith—Jesus Christ. I want to live like the wise man who built his house and his life on a rock.

Today I wisely choose to grow and become all that God has planned that I become.

APRIL 18   AUTHORITY

Now when Jesus had finished saying these things, the crowds were astounded. —Matthew 7:28

Why were Jesus' teachings astounding? The rabbis before Jesus had validated their teachings by citing prophets and other religious leaders. But Jesus needed no authority other than himself. Jesus' words of truth stand alone. Jesus did not seek permission or approval. He boldly set forth to speak and do God's will.

I, too, speak clearly about what I feel and believe. I do not drop names or use other people to make myself feel or appear important. My words are grounded in who I am as a follower of Jesus, and I make no apology for them.

This day, and every day, I accept the authority given to me in Jesus Christ.

APRIL 19   EXPECTATION

When Jesus had come down from the mountain,
great crowds followed him.   —Matthew 8:1

I now take inventory of these past days, and
I am pleased with what I see. I am making an
honest effort to put Jesus first in my life. I am
treating myself and others with more respect.
I am less judgmental and more loving with
myself and with others. And each day, without fear, I am looking for new possibilities and
exciting ways for Jesus to work in and through
my life.

I have met obstacles in these days, and I
have done my best in each situation. I am
learning how to overcome obstacles in a
healthy way. More important, I am learning to
visualize the road home and ask God for guidance and wisdom in the problem areas.

With a keen sense of anticipation, I look for-
ward to what is to come, knowing that with
the help of my risen Savior I can make a safe
journey home.

APRIL 20   RENEWAL

"The kingdom of heaven is like a mustard seed that someone took and sowed in his field; it is the smallest of all the seeds, but when it has grown it is the greatest of shrubs and becomes a tree, so that the birds of the air come and make nests in its branches."
—Matthew 13:31-32

With a fresh start I begin again today. The winter has been long, but a new season looms bright in the future. I allow lightness and a fresh outlook to replace the burdens of yesterday. Like the mustard seed, what I do may begin small, but, as I grow to my intended good, I will be startlingly different from my beginnings.

My ideals are unmet from time to time, but I deal with my anger and do not allow it to fester until I become skeptical. I let go of what I cannot control and look to God to help me move on. I consider new, healthy ways to act in situations that arise. With clear thoughts and ordered feelings, I meet this spring day with renewed energy.

With Jesus Christ in my life, I begin again with an attitude of renewal.

APRIL 21   RENEWAL

"First clean the inside of the cup, so that the outside also may become clean."   —Matthew 23:26

The person I really am inside is reflected in the things I do and say as I interact with my colleagues and family. I do not have to put on a show, masquerading as someone I am not. People like me for who I am.

Today is a good day for spring cleaning the house of my being. I open the windows of my mind and let the fresh air blow in and refresh me with new inspiration. I enter into prayer, and, before God, I discard bitterness, resentment, and sarcasm which no longer fit who I am. I set aside self-criticism and discouraging blame. I scour away the shame.

Into the uncluttered house comes a cool breeze, refreshed with a strong will, joyous laughter, and powerful presence. I'm ready to breathe in the cleansed air and start again. It's time for a new me!

Unencumbered, I feel light with a clean mind and the refreshment of springtime in my step.

—— ❧ ——

APRIL 22   TALENT

To each is given the manifestation of the Spirit for the common good.   —*1 Corinthians 12:7*

I, like others, have been given gifts and talents to be used for the common good of everyone in the community. People appreciate and give credit for my abilities and accomplishments. Likewise, I acknowledge others' talents and feel joy for what they can do. This does not take away from what I can do or be.

I remember that it takes mutual respect to appreciate the unique gift each person brings to the community. I might want to say that some person's abilities are more important than another's due to his or her position or status in life, but God reminds me that we are equally important and that it takes all of us to make a family, organization, or church function fully.

Today I respect the gifts and abilities of myself and others.

The LORD is my shepherd, I shall not want. He makes me lie down in green pastures; he leads me beside still waters; he restores my soul.

—*Psalm 23:1-3a*

As I go about the affairs of my life today, I am aware that God is with me.

In times past, I thought God had deserted me. My own detours in life took me farther away from knowing God's presence, which made me feel alone and abandoned. But this day I know that God is with me and will not desert me. When difficult times come, I am reassured that God will be present to give assurance and comfort.

Today I envision God who watches me and holds me. I let go of fear and anxiety and remember the living presence of God in my life.

I walk through this day assured and untroubled, for I have a God who cares for me and gives me the strength I need.

O sing to the LORD a new song; sing to the LORD, all the earth. Sing to the LORD, bless his name; tell of his salvation from day to day.   —Psalm 96:1-2

Day by day I am learning to sing a new song. I am open to the wonder of life—to new possibilities and ways of doing things. Each day I release my old, inflexible ways and adjust to new attitudes that accommodate unexpected possibilities.

Life is full of different experiences and interesting people. I'm learning to trust myself and be more flexible to meet the potential of the day. I can cope, and live creatively, whatever comes my way.

Today, as I sing a new song, I possess within me the ability to be spontaneous and alive. My life takes on a song of well-being and contentment as I learn to be flexible and open to God's new possibilities.

Today I find joy in exploring the wonder of life.

Live your life in a manner worthy of the gospel of Christ, so that . . . I will know that you are standing firm in one spirit, striving side by side with one mind for the faith. —Philippians 1:27

I live my life in ways that do not neglect the good news of Jesus Christ. This means I live a life that is balanced and allows me to nurture myself and my relationships with friends, family, and other Christians.

In the past I used my job as a way of protecting myself from facing my feelings or dealing with relationships at home. I may need to change my work habits so that I do not compromise my relationships to God and those whom I care about. I need to be able to separate myself from my employment so that I have enough energy to maintain other important parts of my life.

I am defined by both my work and my play. I take an inventory of my spiritual, emotional, and relational life to see if changes need to take place. I am creating a balanced life.

I am creating a future that reflects all of who I am, both in work and in play.

APRIL 26   EXPECTATION

*This one thing I do: forgetting what lies behind and
striving forward to what lies ahead, I press on.*
—*Philippians 3:13-14*

I give myself permission to leave what is
behind and strike out whole-heartedly for the
future. I have the confidence and the perseverance necessary to use the gifts and talents God
has given me to make an important contribu-
tion in whatever realm I choose.

In the past, negative voices told me I could
not succeed. I listened to them, taping them
for instant replay. Now I no longer sabotage
myself by replaying unhelpful tapes. I remove
these barriers and allow my creative nature to
be open for splendid accomplishment.

I believe in myself and my ability to give
my very best. I close the book on yesterday
and focus on this bright new day. Equipped
with a fresh perspective, I am now free to put
my energy into living fully today.

**Today I live in the present to fulfill God's pur-
pose for me.**

We must no longer be children, tossed to and fro and blown about by every wind of doctrine, by people's trickery, by their craftiness in deceitful scheming. But speaking the truth in love, we must grow up in every way into him who is the head, into Christ.
—*Ephesians 4:14-15*

Today I relate to others as a person who has strong convictions. Because I am a person of self-worth with great inner strength, I am not tossed to and fro by what other people say. I no longer have the desperate need to gain everyone's approval. God's stamp of approval is most authentic to me.

How I am feeling and acting are important for me to recognize. If acting in assured ways does not feel authentic to me, I work through the dissonance until I sense inside and out that the act fits what I know about myself. As I learn to love and understand myself for who I am, and others for who they are, I do not need to please everyone in order to gain approval.

Today I stand firm in my convictions.

APRIL 28   *TRUTH*

So then, putting away falsehood, let all of us speak the truth to our neighbors, for we are members of one another.   —Ephesians 4:25

Today I put away all falsehoods. No longer will I pretend that I am someone I am not, or try to cover up mistakes, or refuse to admit when I'm wrong, or tell only half of the story, omitting important details. I accept my mistakes and lack of perfection. Giving myself permission to be wrong means I don't have to judge myself harshly when I fail to meet my own expectations. I forgive myself for errors, past and present, and ask God for forgiveness.

I learn from my mistakes. Some lessons I never will forget and will apply now and in the future. I do not need to cover up past or present mistakes by lying or creating false impressions. The truth is within me. Knowing this, I can face my mistakes and, when possible and appropriate, take action.

Today I interact in truthful ways with the people I encounter.

"If you continue in my word, you are truly my disciples; and you will know the truth, and the truth will make you free."
—John 8:31b-32

I long for the truth necessary for me to live as a disciple of Jesus. Today I seek the truth that sets me free from the bondage of falsehood, which has entrapped me in addiction and sin. As I seek this truth I pray for wisdom to think before I act.

In the past I made decisions impulsively. But today I weigh all the facts and possibilities before making a decision to act. I am not swayed by what others think I should do, but I take into consideration what they say. I take the time to listen to the Holy Spirit within me before I make my best decision.

I make decisions consistent with the true freedom that comes only through Christ.

---❦---

APRIL 30   SELF-ACCEPTANCE

*For now we see in a mirror, dimly, but then we will
see face to face. Now I know only in part; then I will
know fully, even as I have been fully known.*
                                        —1 Corinthians 13:12

When I look in the mirror, I see a person
with both strengths and needs. I recognize
that my needs emerge from my yearning to
grow in power and purpose. My strengths
come from nurturing and caring for others as
well as myself.

As I love others, I am also able to receive
love. When I do acts of kindness or speak
words of praise to others, I bask in the warmth
of this self-giving.

I hold my mirror to look at myself in a clear
light, so the image I see is realistic. I do not
hold a warped mirror, which would create the
distorted image that I am *all* strengths or *all*
needs. There are many dimensions to who I
am. As I gaze, I see and accept all so I can
grow more open to being the person God calls
me to be.

**Today I may only see dimly, yet I continue to
strive to know myself fully.**

If I speak in the tongues of mortals and of angels, but do not have love, I am a noisy gong or a clanging cymbal. And if I have prophetic powers, and understand all mysteries and all knowledge, and if I have all faith, so as to remove mountains, but do not have love, I am nothing. If I give away all my possessions, and if I hand over my body so that I may boast, but do not have love, I gain nothing.

—1 Corinthians 13:1-3

Today I begin to put into action what I have learned. Through my reading, listening, and studying I have acquired much knowledge about my life and how I am to live as a disciple of Jesus Christ. Now I ask myself how I am using my knowledge in my daily life.

Today I transform my personal theories of what needs to be done into practical experiences. It is better for me to put into practice one deed of love than to sit and do nothing. All the information, knowledge, and data I have amount to nothing if I am not committed to action.

Today I risk performing one act of love.

Do you not know that in a race the runners all compete, but only one receives the prize? Run in such a way that you may win it. —*1 Corinthians 9:24*

What are the goals and prizes I seek in life?

In the past I lived a day-to-day existence and settled for a life of comfort and security. I was self-centered because I needed all my energy to simply survive. I acknowledge this past and now move on to lead a fuller life.

When I am unsure of direction, I take time out to pray and ask God for guidance to gain new insights and inspiration. I am challenged to have many experiences and live life in its fullest. Based on past experiences, I am able to form goals that are in keeping with my abilities and interests.

I am not discouraged but consistently move on to achieve my goals.

I know that God inspires me as I work toward my goals.

MAY 3 **PRAYER**

Now during those days he went out to the mountain to pray; and he spent the night in prayer to God.
—*Luke 6:12*

Today I surrender to God in prayer. I trust myself enough to listen to God. I do not block the working of the Holy Spirit in and through me, but I'm open to grow in strength and love. When I am in tune with the Spirit's work, my inner voices are calm and I feel confident and at peace. I am able to love myself and to live in gentle ways, directing caring actions toward others.

Sometimes my thought patterns grow cluttered and my sense of purpose becomes fuzzy and unclear. When I feel this way, I need to pause and determine why. It is important to make an appointment to sit in silence with God and listen carefully. I do not let my ego get in the way but step aside and permit God to act fully.

As I set my own cluttered agenda aside, I allow God to work in my life in deeper ways than I could ever do on my own.

"Blessed are you who weep now, for you will laugh."
—*Luke 6:21*b

Laughter is an important part of my day. I am aware of my growing health and wholeness, and I am alive with delight. I appreciate God's gift of laughter which lifts my load and lightens my heart.

I reflect on the joy I see around me—in children's play, in the midst of absurd situations, and even in the pleasures I receive from the rain that falls or the sun that shines. Laughter is music to my soul which lightens the work of the day. When tension builds, laughter and humor bring release and repose.

Humorous moments come when I, and the people around me, recognize the silly strangeness in some unexpected moment and appreciate the joyful present. My humor is an integral part of who I am and expresses my balanced style of living.

Today I am happy and look for opportunities to laugh. Laughter is a contagion I can share with others.

I rejoice in laughter as an integral part of my life.

— 🍎 —

The LORD answer you in the day of trouble! The name of the God of Jacob protect you!   —Psalm 20:1

Chaos is all around me. I know this when I feel overwhelmed, muddled, and confused. In the past I was caught up in other people's agendas. I found myself caught in the cross-fire between my parents, my children, or my colleagues. I stayed in unhealthy relationships which only defeated my own sense of power.

Today I have the ability to find clarity in the midst of chaos. I am able to quiet my thoughts and see situations clearly. When I am called to make a decision, I slow down, weigh the pros and cons, and come to sound decisions with which I can live today and tomorrow.

Dilemmas are a normal part of each day. I treat them as such and take the time I need to find the quietness of God's Spirit which sustains me.

I am calm and my decisions today reflect my serenity.

---

*You have turned my mourning into dancing; you
have taken off my sackcloth and clothed me with joy,
so that my soul may praise you and not be silent.*
                                                —*Psalm 30:11*

Dancing with joy gives praise and glory to
God. Such joyous expression frees my spirit to
delight in the day God has set before me.
There is great possibility in this day, and I live
it to the fullest. I laugh, sing a little, and dance.

In the past I went through some very dark
days when I thought I would never dance
again. Now I reflect on those days and know
that they have been important to my growth
and development and that they have given me
information that may be used in future decision making. I do not agonize over those days
but accept them as part of my history.

With God as my helper I weather the
storms and turn the grief of yesterday into the
dancing of today. I swirl and turn and move
with a spring in my step.

I dance in the light of this day of promise.

I sought the LORD, and he answered me, and delivered me from all my fears. —Psalm 34:4

Challenges come my way today, and I am ready to meet them wholeheartedly. I am optimistic that the people and opportunities I encounter add to the richness of my experience. These opportunities expand my horizons and stir the gifts within me. God wants my greatest good in all that happens today.

I walk through this day unthreatened by people and situations. I am open and do not anticipate change with fear and dread. I'm positive in my approach to each challenge that today brings. I appreciate the ways I have grown and changed. I choose to live in bold, new ways, celebrating my ability to be awake to all that will enter my life today.

With boldness I step forward to meet today's challenges.

MAY 8   DECISIONS

Show by your good life that your works are done with gentleness born of wisdom. —James 3:13b

I have wisdom as I use sound judgment in today's decision making. I use sound judgment which incorporates my past history and present circumstances. I deal with my feelings and thoughts in mature ways.

Others' judgments do not disrupt my calmness of mind. Negative thoughts, people, and situations do not upset me; I can think with clarity and sharpness.

Today I set aside all false assumptions which interfere with my good judgment, and I deal with what I know is factual and real. This day I stand on a foundation of truth. I ask God for wisdom and discernment as I strive to live as a truthful and faithful disciple of Jesus.

With God as my guide, I make decisions today based on sound judgment.

Let the words of my mouth and the meditation of my heart be acceptable to you, O LORD, my rock and my redeemer.
—*Psalm 19:14*

Today I give myself messages that are positive, definite, and clear. I listen to myself and take time to sort out mixed messages that I receive. I have a responsibility to keep my messages in order and conduct my life in harmony with them.

Sometimes I have to set aside all the extraneous garbage and ask "What is the bottom line?" There are some standards that are not negotiable. I recognize these and stand firm on my values and morals. As a disciple of Jesus Christ, I know where my boundaries are and keep them intact by the decisions I make.

I hear the wisdom of God in my life and listen to it. I take responsibility for the messages I play and move to change those that are negative and unhelpful.

With God as my guide, I take charge of my internal messages and live in harmony, holiness, and peace.

"The kingdom of heaven is like yeast that a woman took and mixed in with three measures of flour until all of it was leavened."   —Matthew 13:33

I anticipate God's will working in my life, like yeast working in flour, giving it new qualities. I am a creative person, unafraid to accept God's possibilities. I daily discover powers and ideas that release my imagination in new ways.

I have many resources to draw upon. I trust my God-given abilities as I move into new arenas. I work for the good of all people in my church and community, including myself. God is transforming me and leading me to new heights of freedom. This freedom allows me to use my best abilities in all I undertake.

Today I am open to God's possibilities.

MAY 11   SELF-ACCEPTANCE

"Consider the ravens: they neither sow nor reap, they have neither store-house nor barn, and yet God feeds them. Of how much more value are you than the birds!"
                            —Luke 12:24

As a part of God's creation, I rejoice in my uniqueness. I choose to acknowledge that I am valued and special. Today I applaud my abilities and talents and rejoice using them to bring glory to Jesus Christ.

I have a clear sense of my self-worth and am true to myself as I interact with others. Because I am unique, I may see things differently than other people. I can easily and generously express my views and opinions. I acknowledge that at times I may be mistaken, and I take responsibility to make corrections or amends.

I also respect others' differences. They too are unique and bring special gifts and talents in their work and play. Both I and my associates are able to claim our own abilities and rejoice.

I value what is unique in me as a follower of Jesus Christ.

A harvest of righteousness is sown in peace for those who make peace.   —James 3:18

Down deep I thirst and hunger for a resting place. I search for peace in the midst of the chaos of this day.

Questions arise within me. What is it that I want from life? What am I presently doing with my life? Do I invest my time in worthy ways? I move to a place of quiet prayer. I meditate and think about these questions.

As I move once again into the activity of the day, my spirit is refreshed. I continue with my day, at peace with myself and my God. I do not expect all the answers today but live gently with the questions.

Today I sit quietly and center myself in peace.

Why are you cast down, O my soul, and why are you disquieted within me? Hope in God; for I shall again praise him, my help and my God.

—*Psalm 42:11*

God created me to be joyful and content, even when living through trials or hard times. I no longer pretend to be happy, making a big display of smiles and hugs while feeling desolate inside. Now I seek real joy through hope in God, which enables me to work for happiness in my relationships and experiences.

I seek persons with whom I enjoy spending time. I choose jobs that give me fulfillment and fill roles in organizations where I am valued. I worship in a church that recognizes and esteems my unique gifts. All these things are expressions of my hope which feed my happiness.

With a spring in my step and lightness of heart, I set out to be happy this day.

MAY 14   PATIENCE

Wait for the LORD; be strong, and let your heart take courage; wait for the LORD!   —Psalm 27:14

Today I will not rush to act before I think. I will allow myself time to weigh carefully all available information before making a decision.

I will take others' actions or opinions into my data bank, but they will not push me to take action before the time is right. When I am impatient, I make hasty decisions. I later wish I had given myself the time to arrive at a different decision.

Today I will be aware of my own sense of timing and listen to my own inner wisdom. As needed, I will ask God for patience, remembering that my time is not necessarily God's time. To seek sound solutions, I will listen and wait.

Today I take time to allow solutions to evolve in their reasonable season.

And this is my prayer, that your love may overflow more and more with knowledge and full insight to help you to determine what is best.
—*Philippians 1:9-10*a

Today I am better equipped to live in intimacy with another person. I have a deepened self-awareness which leads me to a relationship that is healthy and whole.

I no longer will deceive myself by entering into harmful relationships that cannot fulfill my real needs. I have a greater sense of my own needs and an understanding of my past. I am ready to accept the challenges of true intimacy.

I deserve a relationship that is sustainable, and I work to nurture it to its fullest potential. I do not set up blocks that keep me purposely separated from the person with whom I wish to share an intimate relationship. I recognize the barriers and work in honesty with myself and the other person to alleviate any barriers that falsely divide us.

I am intimate with a special person in my life in ways that move me forward.

MAY 16   COMMUNITY

*Let each of you look not to your own interests, but to
the interests of others.*   —*Philippians 2:4*

Today I give glory to God for the people in
my life. I do not live in isolation, but I am a
member of a community. In this community I
give and receive nurture and care. I need companions for the journey, and they need me.

I also seek God for my journey. When I
think I don't need God and can do it all
myself, I am mistaken. I am a human who is
fallible. Today I invite God to enter the events
of my life as I seek to live in community with
others.

**Today I rejoice in the community of which I
am part, and I give of myself to others.**

It is God who is at work in you, enabling you both to will and to work for his good pleasure.

—Philippians 2:13

I am a person with a full and fascinating life, yet there are moments when I find myself longing for a closer connection to what was here before I inhabited this space and what will exist long after I'm gone from this planet.

Today I take time to reconnect, time to ask *real* questions. As I awaken I discover that God exists everywhere in my day-to-day living. I affirm and attend to the profound presence of the Creator in my life as I feed a child, volunteer at the soup kitchen, or visit with an elder. All of these are spiritual actions that bring me closer in touch with my Creator.

I listen to my parched spirit and moisten it with a good dose of truth—truth found in deeds of kindness and acts of charity freely given out of my own sense of purpose.

Today I take the time to be more closely connected to God and others by giving freely of myself.

MAY 18   STRENGTH

I love you, O L̲o̲r̲d̲, my strength. The L̲o̲r̲d̲ is my rock, my fortress, and my deliverer, my God, my rock in whom I take refuge, my shield, and the horn of my salvation, my stronghold.   —Psalm 18:1-2

Today I realize I am part of something larger than myself. I seek God and ask that God "Lead me to a rock that is higher than I." I seek a view of life from a higher rock.

I once knew where my rock was, but somewhere on my journey I stepped down from the rock and lost that vantage point. I got too tense, too busy, too tired, too harried. I was unhappy because I was out of sync with God's purpose.

Now I see clearly again from my place upon the rock of God. I find comfort and strength in knowing that I am safe upon the rock that is higher than I.

Today I look again to the rock of my salvation.

MAY 19 LOVE

Love is patient; love is kind; love is not envious or boastful or arrogant or rude. It does not insist on its own way; it is not irritable or resentful; it does not rejoice in wrongdoing, but rejoices in the truth. It bears all things, believes all things, hopes all things, endures all things. Love never ends.

—*1 Corinthians 13:4-8a*

I praise God for all the love that surrounds me. Because I live in God's love, each day I can love others.

I choose only loving, positive actions today. I have gentleness and love for God, family, friends, and associates. I pass a friendly smile to those I meet, and I am awake and alert to God's world around me. I am poised, and I walk through this day with my head held high in confidence.

Today I am learning to receive love joyfully, without feeling unworthy. I am learning about my own needs and how to give as well as receive.

Today I walk gently in love.

MAY 20   COMMUNICATING

"Out of the abundance of the heart the mouth speaks."
—Matthew 12:34b

As I communicate with people today I do so directly, letting the others know the true feelings in my heart.

"I'm sorry" is a phrase that will not automatically spring to my lips in order to ward off anticipated harm. My insistence on being wrong, exhibited in my need to apologize, is a defensive manner I use even when there is no realistic reason for me to placate. This sort of self-abasement only annoys people. I, too, grow weary of my rush to assume blame and guilt.

As a child "I'm sorry" was a ritual expression used to bring painful episodes to a close. But saying "I'm sorry" to someone almost without thinking has never helped me understand why what I've done is wrong.

I no longer automatically apologize because I fear a person's anger or retaliation. The words "I'm sorry" are reserved for times when I am at fault.

I communicate today with power.

MAY 21   *FEAR*

Jesus came and touched them, saying, "Get up and do not be afraid."
                                    —*Matthew 17:7*

Today I no longer live in fear. I have been touched by the one who tells me to "Get up and do not be afraid." Sometimes it's hard to get up in the morning, knowing what I must face, and not be somewhat fearful.

In times past there were days I thought I'd never survive. I look back now and see that I have survived and, in many ways, even flourished. Experience tells me that I can let go of the responsibility to change other people and move out of tense situations that can't be changed.

Calmness is at the center of my day. As I challenge myself to conquer fear, new heights of inner strength and determination are within my reach.

I look to Jesus today and urge my fears away.

MAY 22   SAFETY

"Every kingdom divided against itself is laid waste, and no city or house divided against itself will stand."   —*Matthew 12:25*b

Today I live in my house in safety. My home is a haven where I am happy and free to be accepted and loved.

Anger and aggression in the form of subtle jabs and inconsistencies no longer are the norm. Now I consciously surround myself with strength, acceptance, and gentleness. I have freedom to be who I want to be. There are no false expectations laid upon me. If changes need to be made, I confront them directly. If people need to be called into accountability, I do it gently but directly. A large dose of love is at the center of everything said and done in my house.

I have a place where I can rest and be at ease.

*For God so loved the world that he gave his only Son,
so that everyone who believes in him may not perish
but may have eternal life.*   —*John 3:16*

As today dawns, I am reminded of God's
love for the world and the miracle of Jesus'
coming. The reality of the eternal truth is that
in Christ we are one.

Today I cast aside the darkness that hides
the truth. I allow God's love to radiate
through my life. I emerge from darkness into
God's light, which guides me in the ways that
are full of truth.

Today I am aware of God's presence within
me. I have a sense of wonder as I watch
glimpses of God's new world unfolding. I treat
today, and every day, as a fresh beginning.
When evening comes and the moon appears in
the sky, I take a quick inventory of my experiences of this day and use these learnings as
part of tomorrow's promise for a better world
for myself and all God's people.

**I continue to explore the awesomeness of
God's love for the world through Jesus Christ.**

MAY 24   TRIALS

Truly God is good to the upright, to those who are pure in heart. But as for me, my feet had almost stumbled; my steps had nearly slipped.

—*Psalm 73:1-2*

I may not always be "pure in heart," but I try to be. God nurtures me in love, wisdom, and truth. I have a steady faith that takes whatever problems come today and makes them opportunities for growth. I find fulfillment in tackling difficult situations and finding resolve. I rejoice and give God thanks today for my numerous opportunities.

There is orderliness and calm in my life. Each minute, hour, and day passes in the assurance of serenity. As each new situation presents itself, I discover a depth of wisdom and new understanding about myself and other people. No matter what happened in the past year, month, or week, I move through today secure in an awareness that nothing can separate me from God's love and goodness. Today does not present problems but opportunities.

I rejoice in the sturdiness that leads me through difficult times with sure footing.

MAY 25   STRENGTH

O God, from my youth you have taught me, and I still proclaim your wondrous deeds. So even to old age and gray hairs, O God, do not forsake me.
—*Psalm 71:17-18*a

From the time of my youth and through my old age, God is with me. It is good to know that even as change occurs in my life God is a constant companion. People come and go, I move from city to city, circumstances and events change, but God is always there for me.

All these days are mine to use in wisdom, joy, and delight. My life is a divine gift. My health, my speech, my thoughts, and my actions point to God, who has been my constant teacher. As I remember God's presence, I am set free from all tension and stress and find strength and reassurance. I am conscious that God continues to be present with me today as in the past.

As I move into more mature years, I know from past experiences that God continues to be present and to give me strength.

MAY 26   HARMONY

And whatever you do, in word and deed, do every-
thing in the name of the Lord Jesus, giving thanks to
God the Father through him. —*Colossians 3:17*

My words (what I say) and my deeds (what I actually end up doing) match. I thank God that I am no longer divided against myself by living one way and professing something else.

I feel the harmony that comes to me when I live the life of a disciple of Jesus in both word and deed. When I take time to remind myself that God is guiding my journey, I feel peaceful and tranquil.

Today I am true to my word as much as possible. If my words and my actions do not correspond, I confess my failure to whomever has been wronged and then work to reconcile the situation. I live as a disciple of Jesus Christ in both word and deed.

Today I live in word and deed for the glory of Christ.

"I am the good shepherd. I know my own and my own know me."   *—John 10:14*

I have a good shepherd who loves me and is with me always. My shepherd knows me by name. Nothing is hidden, for the shepherd knows me through and through. Because this shepherd watches over me, I can live in calm and peace. I can separate myself from the stresses in my life's daily schedule and handle all that confronts me with calm and gentleness.

Knowing that I have a shepherd who watches with me, I take charge and define my boundaries and direction. I claim my power, and renewed energy surges through me. Children, bosses, colleagues, and projects will not overtake me. I realistically set goals and limits and live within them.

Because I know my shepherd, Jesus, I walk through this day in peace.

Martha said to Jesus, "Lord, if you had been here, my brother would not have died. But even now I know that God will give you whatever you ask of him." Jesus said to her, "Your brother will rise again."
—John 11:21-23

Today I pause to recall the rich experiences I shared with loved ones who have died and to thank God for their presence in my life. These memories bring happiness and sadness. I've said goodbye, but I sometimes have difficulty accepting the finality of the separation. Sometimes I even feel abandoned by God, as Martha did, and I tell God how I feel.

I know I will see my loved ones again in God's time. This knowledge does not mean I will not feel sadness and loss. I accept these emotions and remind myself of how fortunate I am to have had time with my family members and friends. God blessed me with their lives. I will carry their memory throughout my life.

Today I remember loving people from my past.

"A disciple is not above the teacher, but everyone who is fully qualified will be like the teacher."

—*Luke 6:40*

Today I am both teacher and pupil. I have wisdom, knowledge, and understanding, which I share with others. Others have things to teach me, and I am eager to learn from them. I learn and relearn throughout my life as I remain open to the way of discipleship. I do not condemn myself for mistakes, failings, or inadequacies but expand my vision and understanding as I pay attention, ask questions, and learn from others.

The time is right today to learn to draw or paint, play an instrument, or use a computer. When the timing is right, I will use other untapped capabilities.

I have come a long way on my journey, but I am open to new knowledge and understandings. My mind expands daily to take in all the newness life offers.

I am both teacher and pupil as a disciple of Jesus.

MAY 30   PEACE

And let the peace of Christ rule in your hearts, to which indeed you were called in the one body. And be thankful.   —Colossians 3:15

I have peace within my heart which cannot be taken from me. I accept that I cannot fully know how my path will intertwine with the larger scheme of God's plan, but I trust God to see me through the journey.

Many times I have prayed for things I have wanted or needed. My prayers have not been in vain, for when things have not happened as I have wanted, I have changed to meet the challenge of the situation. Sometimes what I pray for changes, and sometimes I change.

When I'm disappointed, I find unexpected learnings. I am constantly on the road to new discoveries about myself and God's world. I have had my share of suffering, but through these hard times I have awakened to an understanding I otherwise might have missed.

I have peace within as I learn to trust myself and God.

—— 🍂 ——

May you be made strong with all the strength that comes from his glorious power, and may you be prepared to endure everything with patience, while joyfully giving thanks to the Father, who has enabled you to share in the inheritance of the saints in the light.   —Colossians 1:11-12

I feel good about myself today. I know that up and down shifts in self-esteem are perfectly normal—and temporary. Most downward shifts right themselves almost effortlessly. Some linger like a stubborn virus. But I am secure enough to roll with the punches.

When a downward shift in self-esteem comes, I take time to look at unfinished emotional business of the past and stay attuned to what my feelings are telling me. When I get a good report, gain a new friend, or get a promotion, I enjoy these pleasures and allow them to undergird me in the rough times. I maintain a basic sense of self-worth that sees me through the good times and the bad.

I have strength and endurance because I know who I am—a saint of God!

JUNE 1   RELATIONSHIPS

You do well if you really fulfill the royal law according to the scripture, "You shall love your neighbor as yourself."
               —James 2:8

As I continue to grow, I find the courage to discontinue unhealthy relationships with people who are overly critical and do not accept me as I am. I fill my world with people who respect themselves and therefore have a caring respect and consideration for me, too.

It is liberating to realize that some people simply are incapable of the love and approval I require. Their inabilities have nothing to do with me. I let go of the anger and resentment I've felt toward them and accept them for who they are. I don't expect them to offer a relationship that is beyond their capabilities.

I am happier and more content in my relationships. I care for and have respect for the people in my life, and I expect the same in return. I do not settle for less.

I liberate myself and find new freedom as I work realistically within my relationships.

JUNE 2   JOY

Make a joyful noise to the LORD, all the earth.
—*Psalm 100:1*

I delight in fully experiencing this day. I do not want to miss one moment. All my senses are awake to the beauty of life, and I am conscious of the possibilities of the vital work before me. Today I celebrate the wonderful joy around me.

Small children enjoy small pleasures and find life fascinating. Picking a dandelion, watching the ants on the sidewalk, or splashing in a mud puddle are times of laughter and wonderment. Just because I am growing older does not mean I must miss the everyday pleasures of life. I lose an important part of who I am when I forget to allow the child within me to live and love.

Today I take time to glide down a slide, feed the birds, and climb the rocks. The joy of simple fun that I had as a child still lives within me. I celebrate my child!

I am a joyful, creative person who has the ability to recapture all the good in what it means to be a child.

"Strive to enter through the narrow door; for many, I tell you, will try to enter and will not be able."
—Luke 13:24

There are doors in front of me from which to choose. Some doors, appealingly decorated, invite me to walk through them. I may choose to walk through these beckoning doors, but I need to recognize that they may lead me to unhealthy or even destructive places.

Christ urges me to open the door marked Life. This door leads to a path that, in the beginning, is hard to walk. I must forget old ways of living and overcome destructive patterns before I can take control of my life as a disciple of Jesus.

Today I walk with confidence saying: "No more fighting," "No more blaming," and "No more bitter arguments." Instead, as I journey farther down this road, I find acceptance, acknowledgment, and peace. The door I choose leads to serenity with myself and others.

I choose to walk the road of a disciple of Jesus.

God is light and in him there is no darkness at all. If we say that we have fellowship with him while we are walking in darkness, we lie and do not do what is true.   —*1 John 1:5-6*

Day by day I look for God's light and truth. I know the secret of cultivating true faith is taking time for meditation and prayer. I renew my belief in Jesus Christ by studying, reading, and spending time with other supportive disciples who are also learning to walk in the light.

When I walk in the light of faith, I vanquish my fears. In Christ's light I find the strength to survive the difficult times.

I refuse to walk in darkness anymore. I walk in darkness when I lie to myself and my loved ones. I walk in darkness when I compromise myself in order to please others. I walk in darkness when I allow myself to go through days numb, rather than recognizing my anger and taking action. I am a person of light and faith, and I will live accordingly.

Today I walk in the light.

Be doers of the word, and not merely hearers who deceive themselves.   —James 1:22

Today I am a "doer." I affect my decisions by writing in my journal what I choose. With care I choose thoughts and put them into sentences that are full of peace and joy. On each page I erase negative thoughts and replace them with thoughts that are healthy, creative, and productive.

Line by line I am becoming a new person full of ability, insight, and wisdom. I set aside archaic beliefs and compose new poetry that speaks of my growth-producing beliefs and behaviors.

I pause before I write to decide what I want. I consider what God wants me to do with my life. I encounter this day with renewed confidence in my ability to change.

In the days to come my journal will be filled with healthy, creative, and productive stories of my new life.

 🍎

For everything created by God is good, and nothing is to be rejected, provided it is received with thanksgiving.
—*1 Timothy 4:4*

My body is important, and I want to maintain its health. In the past my physical body became the psychological battleground for difficulties in my life. Today I quiet the inner voices that criticize my body.

When I feel angry, depressed, powerless, or inadequate, I am especially hard on myself. I look at my physical appearance with distaste and loathe what I see. I want to change my height, my weight, my entire physical look. To nullify this self-hate I quickly turn to crash diets or excessive exercise. Neither helps me to be a healthier person.

I realize that my body is not the basis of my conflict. I will stop abusing and neglecting my physical self because this will not solve my inner problems or unresolved emotions. I will learn to live out my emotions in more direct ways and to face the situation realistically.

I am thankful for my body, and I show my thanks by taking care of myself.

JUNE 7   *POWER*

I will study the way that is blameless. When shall I attain it? I will walk with integrity of heart within my house.
         —Psalm 101:2

Trying to be blameless is not easy, especially when I allow my anger to grow and grow until it takes over my life. I must walk with integrity and claim the power to right the injustices in my life.

My anger often springs from my feelings of powerlessness. It's painful to admit that sometimes the only solution to a bad situation is to walk away from it. My self-directed anger allows me to think that if I only started doing something right, the other person or situation would improve. I set myself up as the victim and blame myself instead of seeing the reality of the situation. I now realize that this recurring pattern leaves me feeling angry, hurt, and helpless.

Today I claim the power I have to make changes in the circumstances of my life. Assertively, I make choices to realistically assess the situation and act accordingly.

I walk with integrity of heart within my house.

JUNE 8   HARMONY

O sing to the LORD a new song, for he has done mar-
velous things. . . . Make a joyful noise to the LORD,
all the earth.   —Psalm 98:1a, 4

Today I sing a new song. I stand at the
podium and conduct my own choir. As I lead I
am creative, disciplined, and organized. I
know the song score, and I flow free with its
notes.

In the past there were many conductors in
my life. I let my parents, friends, or teachers
lead. They told me that they knew what was
best for me. They raised their batons and com-
peted for my attention to their songs.

Today I sing the song the way I know God
is leading me to sing it. I decide if I will sing
soprano, alto, tenor, or base. I orchestrate my
spiritual and physical well being to create a
new harmony in this day. I enjoy the beautiful
balance of sound that is created.

I listen and hear God's music and restore bal-
ance and harmony to my life.

JUNE 9   THANKFULNESS

In our prayers for you we always thank God, the Father of our Lord Jesus Christ, for we have heard of your faith in Christ Jesus and of the love that you have for all the saints.   —Colossians 1:3-4

Today I think of the people I appreciate and tell them so. I am able to praise and give thanks for their presence in my life. Their faith in God encourages me to continue on my own faith journey.

I show my appreciation to others as I fully appreciate myself. At this moment I think of myself in the finest terms. So, too, I remember the best in other people.

Gradually I am learning to think good thoughts about myself, my friends, and my loved ones. Especially when I pray, I take the time to thank God for these "saints" in my life. I also thank God for me.

Today I am thankful for all the wonderful people who have blessed my day.

Then Jesus answered her, "Woman, great is your faith! Let it be done for you as you wish." And her daughter was healed instantly.   *—Matthew 15:28*

Faith is a power that is experienced through life's full wonder and glory. I cannot call upon someone else's faith or live by another person's beliefs. To strengthen my faith I must use it, or it will wither.

As I grow in faith in God, I also grow in belief in myself. New possibilities open to me as my belief in myself grows stronger. Faith in God and belief in myself are like electric light currents. Unless I allow them to flow through my life, I remain in darkness. The electricity is there all the time, but I must get out of its way and allow the current to flow through the circuits.

Today I practice my faith. I have faith that God is active in my life, and I use the strength this presence gives to my everyday living.

I live in my faith in Jesus Christ which gives clarity to my life today.

"The kingdom of heaven may be compared to a king who gave a wedding banquet for his son."

—Matthew 22:2

I feast at the banquet that Christ has laid out for me today. I do not make excuses for why I cannot attend or enjoy the feast. I have a choice. Life in Jesus Christ can be a five-course dinner; each course can be filling, delicious, and wonderful. Or I can settle for a diet of fast foods, which only temporarily satisfy my hunger.

Jesus tells me that to enjoy the feast I must be willing to develop a taste for some new foods. All that I eat may not be familiar to my taste buds, but I can rejoice and find joy in the experience.

No longer will I starve myself by saying I am not good enough. I will not stay away for fear of unknown people who might be seated at the table. Jesus has a place set for me, and I will join the feast.

I choose to partake in the feast of life today.

JUNE 12   GUILT

*From his fullness we have all received, grace upon
grace.*   —John 1:16

Today I give myself credit for the good
things I do. If I make a mess of something, I
claim God's grace rather than jump to the
conclusion that I can't do anything right.

When guilt is justified, I face up to it, apologize to those I've hurt, and do my best to
make amends. The longer I avoid recognizing
my sin and acknowledging my guilt, the
worse I'll feel. If there is no possibility of setting things right with the other person, I ask
God for forgiveness and work to avoid making
the same mistake in the future.

Sometimes I ask myself, "Why *should* I stay
indoors to catch up on work on the first sunny,
warm spring day?" or "Why *should* I habitually
take the extra jobs at work?"

Today I make a conscious decision to separate the "shoulds" I want to keep from those
that serve only as unnecessary sources of guilt.
I am able to take advantage of the opportunities for learning and growth by acknowledging
my guilt while avoiding the tendency to feel
overwhelmed by remorse and worthlessness.

**I claim God's grace and take whatever action I
can to alleviate the cause of my guilt.**

JUNE 13   *FORGIVENESS*

Then Peter came and said to him, "Lord, if another member of the church sins against me, how often should I forgive? As many as seven times?" Jesus said to him, "Not seven times, but, I tell you, seventy-seven times."   —Matthew 18:21-22

Today I concentrate on forgiveness and remove the resentment that inhibits my well-being. Jesus knew that resentment takes energy that can be used for healthy purposes. Unforgiving rage blocks my spiritual peace and affects me emotionally and physically.

I no longer allow resentment to grow and fester. I no longer allow my lack of forgiveness to control my life. Today I release my rage and forgive people I resent. I know that only through forgiving others will I be able to completely forgive myself. I experience new freedom today as I forgive myself and others who have hurt me.

I ask God to help me forgive people who have hurt me.

Trust in the LORD, and do good. . . . Take delight in the LORD, and he will give you the desires of your heart.   —*Psalm 37:3-4*

Today I take delight in my dreams and desires. I quiet anxious alarms that go off inside my head whenever I dare to dream. Of course, there are desires that are inappropriate or even destructive. I ask God's forgiveness for these desires without putting a guilt trip on myself. I wisely choose not to put some desires into action.

Today I allow dreams and desires to surface. Dreams are a staple of life necessary for growth. The stronger my desires, and the more clearly I see them, the more effective my actions will be.

I evaluate my desires carefully and, as I live a balanced life, share these with God. I trust my decisions about which desires I will attempt to actualize and which dreams I will work to fulfill.

As a disciple of Jesus, I dare to dream boldly and trust myself to make appropriate decisions.

Do you not know that all of us who have been baptized into Christ Jesus were baptized into his death? Therefore we have been buried with him by baptism into death, so that, just as Christ was raised from the dead by the glory of the Father, so we too might walk in newness of life.   —Romans 6:3-4

Discipleship means not just dangling my feet in the waters of the Jordan, but diving in and getting wet all over. Baptism involves all of who I am and offers me a new life in Christ.

In the past I stood safely on the shoreline or clung to a life raft for fear of sinking. But now I know that when I camouflage myself with thin smiles, half-hearted commitments, and superficial words, I counterfeit my life.

Today I have the courage to remove the false securities and life vests which keep me from swimming with powerful strokes. I'm immersed fully in Christ so that I'm not divided within myself.

I step into the water, first getting my feet wet and then my entire body, knowing that Jesus is waiting on the other side of the river.

JUNE 16　　　*SPIRITUAL HEALTH*

It is good to give thanks to the LORD, to sing praises to your name, O Most High; to declare your steadfast love in the morning, and your faithfulness by night.　　　　　　　*—Psalm 92:1-2*

Today I find quiet time to just be, not do. I allow myself to be moved beyond logic and reason to another way of knowing—God's way of knowing. Other times I choose to follow more structured ways of prayer and contemplation. The important aspect is that I commit myself to time with God.

I calm my mind and body and open myself to God's Spirit. I simply observe, and not control, what happens within me. I check my body for tension and slow my breathing so I can relax.

As I relax in this mindful presence before God, I become more spiritually aware. I am alert and perceptive in the present moment.

I take time to be in the presence of God for my spiritual health.

Let me hear what God the LORD will speak, for he will speak peace to his people, to his faithful, to those who turn to him in their hearts.   —Psalm 85:8

Today I redefine prayer and claim its usefulness and importance in my life. As I pray and acknowledge my relationship to God in Jesus Christ, I affirm that I am a person worthy to be talking with my Creator and Savior.

I begin to pray and get the hang of it. I begin in an unhurried voice to praise God, and I present my prayer in whatever form feels comfortable to me. As I move on in my prayer, I express my sorrow for things I wish I hadn't done and things I've left undone. If there are people in my life whose forgiveness I need, I ask for it now in my prayer. Then I give thanks for the gifts in my life, tangible and intangible. I enumerate them with pleasure and gratitude. Finally, I ask God to help me with the changes I'd like to make in my life.

I pray, knowing that God hears me and impacts my life in real ways.

JUNE 18   REVERENCE

How lovely is your dwelling place, O LORD of hosts!
My heart and flesh sing for joy to the living God.
                                        —*Psalm 84:1-2*

Today I get in touch with God. One way I do this is to set aside time each day to express the awe I feel when I look at the stars or enjoy the rain. Another way is to serve others who need my abilities. When I'm involved in the needs of the world through volunteer work in my church and community, I am in touch with God.

When I stretch beyond myself I gain new energy, serenity, and even elation. I develop the flexibility to live with ambiguity, paradox, and change because I am balanced, centered, and awake in Christ. I may not have all the answers as I reach toward other people, but I do not expect myself to have them. Instead, I am awe-filled with the richness gained from living the questions.

When I deepen my spiritual life with God, the world, in some way, is a better place. I am in touch with God and contribute to the reverence of God's world.

I am awe-filled by God's touch.

Teach and admonish one another in all wisdom; and with gratitude in your hearts sing psalms, hymns, and spiritual songs to God.

—*Colossians 3:16*b

Today I will not sweat the small stuff. I see the big picture and know what is truly important. As my perspective grows beyond myself, I am able to grasp the larger understanding of God's world and my place in it. I know that my relationships with others enrich my life, but they do not define me.

As I find life's meanings through my relationship with Christ, I no longer define my life by significant others. Today I am free to *want* someone rather than frantically *need* them. I am stronger, more independent, and more likely to insist on being treated well.

As I deepen my spiritual life through Christ, I am happier—even in the midst of pain or misfortune. In this season of my life I wish for myself reverence, discovery, challenge, and warmth in all my relationships.

As I gaze at the big picture, my relationships with others fall into perspective.

JUNE 20   SPIRITUAL HEALTH

O God, you are my God, I seek you, my soul thirsts for you; my flesh faints for you, as in a dry and weary land where there is no water.   —*Psalm 63:1*

Both my soul and my body are in need of God. Today I take the time to erase the boundaries between my spiritual life and my physical life.

I will no longer live with the limiting assumption that the *spiritual* is separate from the *day to day*. When I'm involved in an act that attends to and affirms the profound and right, I am living life in the Spirit. When I prepare a meal for my children or a friend, it is a spiritual action. When I volunteer at a shelter for the homeless or give aid to a stranger, I am in the midst of spiritual practice.

I don't expect instant enlightenment by following a few practical rules or exercises. There is no substitute for the devotion and discipline needed to be a disciple of Jesus. But today I take an important and vital step toward filling my thirst for God.

As I seek God, I know I will find the water that quenches thirst.

---❦---

JUNE 21   SPIRITUAL HEALTH

Lead me to the rock that is higher than I.

—*Psalm* 61:2b

Spirituality is the view of life from a higher rock. On this higher rock I have a broader, clearer perspective of my life.

I knew the view well when I was a child. But as I've grown up, I've stepped down from the rock, losing that vantage point. I get too busy, too bruised, too tense, too tired for a spiritual life. Or subtle societal messages tell me it's unseemly to think or talk of such things.

Now I'm sure I'm part of something larger than myself. Today I consider the issues of deepest meaning: "Why am I here?" and "What is it that God requires of me?" I no longer hold back for fear people will think I'm being too personal, too sentimental, or too silly. I find my spiritual life once again and face the challenge of discovering my sense of meaning, value, and purpose.

I am ready to stand on a higher rock once again and explore the spiritual parts of myself.

For God alone my soul waits in silence, for my hope is from him.
           —*Psalm 62:5*

I find a space of quiet and silence within my busy day to pray and wait for God. There are questions of great importance that I want to explore.

I've found that when I am most unhappy, I am out of sync with God and the spiritual side of myself. It's not that I don't have real problems dealing with job troubles, difficult relatives, or unsettled disputes. But I suffer most when I am in the deeper discomfort that comes from ignoring the source of profound wisdom which comes from God. I may be on the top of the world and my life may be fascinating and full, yet what I consciously or unconsciously long for is a relationship with God.

Today I take the time my spiritual life needs. I do not rob myself of this important part of who I am.

Today I enjoy my spiritual awakening.

⚜

JUNE 23   TALENT

We, however, will not boast beyond limits, but will keep within the field that God has assigned to us.
—*2 Corinthians 10:13a*

I know my limits and live within those limits. This does not mean I do not stretch my talents to live to my full potential, but there are some things I know I cannot do. I am not ashamed to admit where I am inadequate and need help from others. I do not have to pretend to be perfect.

The limits I set for myself and live within are appropriate and realistic. When I treat myself well, I know that I am valuable and worthwhile. I no longer seek another's approval by overshooting my limits. In fact, I am even learning to say no to tasks that would be better left to someone else with the necessary talents and interest.

Today I affirm my abilities and talents and choose work I enjoy that is within my scope. If I decide to try something new, I ask for help as I learn.

Today I live responsibly and do my best in whatever I pursue.

—— ❧ ——

*Religion that is pure and undefiled before God . . .
is this: to care for orphans and widows in their distress, and to keep oneself unstained by the world.*
                                        —James 1:27

Today I will not be overwhelmed by the hungry, homeless, and victimized persons around me. In the past I felt powerless and questioned what one person could do to make a difference. Now I realize that I am not supposed to do it alone.

I am part of a community that works to make a difference. When I join with other people who share a vision of possibility, things can change. God is present wherever people come together to bring about relief, compassion, and justice. I realize that to have a relationship with God I must also be an active participant in community. Today I work in community to take one step toward tackling a problem.

I seek a community of other disciples to right the wrongs.

You have turned my mourning into dancing; you have taken off my sackcloth and clothed me with joy, so that my soul may praise you and not be silent.
—Psalm 30:11-12a

Just for today I give myself fully to living life with gladness and thanksgiving. I experience the dance of life freely. I express my dance physically as I twirl around and as I express love, joy, and enthusiasm.

Today I allow Jesus to shine through with joy and ease. Just as I sway to and fro in dance, so also I give and take to make this day work for me. I relearn old steps I thought I'd long forgotten, and I learn new steps and rhythms which better fit the person I'm becoming.

I move to the music of the maestro, Christ Jesus. Today I relax and allow cheerfulness and good will to be in my steps.

I dance in the joy and beauty of life.

JUNE 26   *HARMONY*

Above all, clothe yourselves with love, which binds everything together in perfect harmony.

—*Colossians 3:14*

Today I clothe myself with love and I find harmony in my relationships. I take pleasure in my own life, and, therefore, I am able to rejoice with or provide support for others.

I no longer bring another down in order to build myself up or engage in whiny resentment toward anyone who seems to have more than their "fair share" of life's blessings. My friends do not have to fail for me to feel successful. I give genuine compliments to my friends because I'm happy for them and the good that comes their way.

I do not put up with people in my life who are unable to rejoice with me. I surround myself with people who are happy for my accomplishments and cheer me on to greater things. In these ways I live in harmony with others.

Today I live in harmony as I affirm the people in my life.

JUNE 27   FORGIVENESS

Bear with one another and, if anyone has a complaint against another, forgive each other; just as the Lord has forgiven you, so you also must forgive.

—Colossians 3:13

Today I tell people when I'm upset with something they've done. I do not place blame but simply tell them how the circumstance made me feel. I no longer play the martyr, swallowing whatever someone dishes out; I speak up for myself.

I recognize when I play the role of martyr that I'm simply inflaming my own sense of injustice. It upsets me when I'm convinced other people are getting more than they deserve or are putting one over on me. I acknowledge when I set up situations that are bound to aggravate my mythical sense of injustice, and I see these self-righteous feelings for what they are—an enormous waste of time and energy. I use all my energy for living with others in healthy, forgiving ways.

Today I forgive others as God has forgiven me.

——— 🍎 ———

JUNE 28   ENVY

So if you have been raised with Christ, ... set your
minds on things that are above, not on things that
are on earth. ... then you also will be revealed with
him in glory.   —*Colossians 3:1-2,* 4b

Today I set my mind on the new me, which
was born in Christ Jesus. I put to rest ways of
acting and thinking that had a passive strangle-
hold on me.

The passivity of envy was one of those
unproductive emotions that held me in its
grasp. I now realize there's a vast difference
between thinking "I can do that, too" and
being the envious person who sits like a lump
thinking "I'll never get that far." I need to recognize that when I put others down, it's I who
has the problem with self-acceptance.

Today I let go of the envy trap, accept
myself for the good person I am, and make an
effort to alter what needs to be changed. I no
longer use envy as a way to express anger or
avoid action. I appreciate myself and my
unique gifts and talents and rejoice in my
friends' and relatives' gifts and talents as well.

Today I rid myself of envy and set my mind
on positive things so I will be revealed with
Christ in glory.

As God's chosen ones, holy and beloved, clothe your-selves with compassion, kindness, humility, meekness, and patience.   —*Colossians 3:12*

As one of God's chosen people, I know I am loved. I cast aside old, worn out clothes which no longer fit the person I am today and put on clothes that show off my new attributes of being a disciple of Jesus. I am compassionate, kind, humble, meek, and patient.

As I am guided by God I choose powerful, strong, loving ideas. I'm continually aware of the power of the Holy Spirit which clothes me with boldness in my actions and attitudes.

In the past I didn't value my thoughts and feelings enough to act on them. I grew more and more indecisive, convinced that my ideas were worthless. Today I value all my thoughts and acknowledge the richness of my ideas. I trust myself to act in right ways as I am led along the path of Christ.

Today I act like the chosen person of God I am.

—— ❦ ——

JUNE 30   ENVY

But fornication and impurity of any kind, or greed, must not even be mentioned among you, as is proper among saints. —*Ephesians 5:3*

As a disciple of Christ I set aside the impurities of greed and envy that keep me in bondage. No longer am I an envious person, feeling diminished by another's achievements or happiness.

Perhaps my envy originated in childhood. It moved far beyond rivalry, competitiveness, and jealousy with my brothers, sisters, or friends to a feeling that there was a limited quantity of love and happiness in the world. I was afraid there wouldn't be enough for me if other people seemed to be getting more than their "fair share."

I no longer act like a child, running around screaming, "It's not fair!" The truth is, life isn't always fair, and sometimes no one is to blame. Of course, I may continue to have feelings of envy and greed. The difference now is that I don't act on them. I fight these impure feelings to bring about my better impulses.

Today I set aside envious talk and sing praises instead.

---❦---

JULY 1   PRAYER

I keep the Lord always before me. . . . Therefore my heart is glad, and my soul rejoices; my body also rests secure.   *—Psalm 16:8-9*

When I begin to feel overwhelmed with pressure, it is time to back off, slow down, and remember that my mental health is very important. Today I make a conscious effort to distance myself from stress and pressure. I allow myself free time to loaf, to notice my surroundings, and to speak to God.

In the past I had to remain always alert and ready to react to whatever family emergency presented itself. Now I take time out for prayer. My prayers are centered on restful interludes, health, and healing. I set aside fifteen minutes today to relax, meditate, and pray. Taking this important time is vital to my spiritual well being.

Today I claim time from my busy day to spend in reflection and meditation with God.

JULY 2   DECISIONS

*As Jesus passed along the Sea of Galilee, he saw
Simon and his brother Andrew casting a net into the
sea. . . . And Jesus said to them, "Follow me and I
will make you fish for people." And immediately they
left their nets and followed him.*   —Mark 1:16-18

Like Simon and Andrew, I have the ability
to think and make good decisions for direction
in my life. Today I pray for guidance as I ask
myself, "What do I think is right for who I
am?"

Sometimes I seek the advice and consulta-
tion of a person I trust. Yet I do so with the
full understanding that I am the one who
makes the final decision. I know if I try to
please everyone, I will probably end up pleasing no one at all, not even myself.

I'm a worthwhile person who makes good
decisions. Today I consciously make decisions
and take full responsibility for those decisions
which lead to my actions.

**I pray for a clear mind to examine situations
as they arise and make the best decisions possible.**

JULY 3   *GRACE*

For by grace you have been saved through faith, and this is not your own doing; it is the gift of God.
—*Ephesians 2:8*

Christ shows grace and blessings in my life just because I am God's child. Just as parents love a child because the child belongs to them, so, too, God loves me. I am a part of Christ's family, and I am pleasing and acceptable to God.

I know that I am lovable and worthy of praise. I set aside all self-blame. Of course, I'm aware of my limitations and know I'll make mistakes, because I am part of humanity which stands in need of God's grace. I confess my sins, asking forgiveness of God and, when needful and appropriate, of others as well. Shame no longer is part of who I am. I acknowledge my faults, seek reconciliation, and move on.

Today I am learning to seek and accept God's grace.

Jesus laid his hands on his eyes again; and he looked intently and his sight was restored, and he saw every-thing clearly.   —Mark 8:25

My sight is clear and I now see with an honest understanding I never knew was possible. Jesus has restored my sight, and I give God thanks.

For years I, like the blind man, walked around half awake. I was too afraid to face reality. Now I rejoice that the blur is gone. I see clearly, and I'm not afraid to name what I see.

If a person betrays me and is not worthy of my trust, I no longer give it. When someone says slanted, cutting remarks, I acknowledge the hurt. I value myself and my relationships too much to simply brush aside unkindnesses. Today I value my new-found sight.

Today my eyes are open, and I see people clearly.

Then he said to me, "It is done! I am the Alpha and the Omega, the beginning and the end. To the thirsty I will give water as a gift from the spring of the water of life."   —Revelation 21:6

Today I invite God to take my hand and lead me to the spring of life. This spring is one of rediscovery—rediscovery of my love and strengths that were so long buried deep within me. I'm able to use my renewed strength and love to choose the streams I wish to swim in —streams bringing health and wholeness. The joy of life-giving water is here, and I drink freely.

Many times I've tried to swim upstream. The current coursed incessantly against me. The water I drank was polluted with my own self-defeating behaviors. Today I learn new ways of swimming that are life-sustaining and that build my strength. I renew my energies and follow streams of joy and peace.

I put my trust in the Alpha and Omega who fills my need and satisfies my thirst.

—— 🍂 ——

JULY 6   TRANSFORMATION

And the one who was seated on the throne said, "See, I am making all things new."   —Revelation 21:5

Today I close the book on past hurts and disappointments, and I look at my successes. The old has passed away, and all things begin anew. When Jesus returns to claim his own, everything will be made new. Yet, even now I can live in new ways as I prepare for Christ's return.

When I was a child, I was told through words and actions that I was a failure. But now I realize I did the best I could. Those memories no longer bind me. I have purpose, and I am learning to live in fulfilling ways. In God I begin today to make everything new.

Today I thank God for making all things new and beautiful in my life.

JULY 7   SUFFERING

*"He will wipe every tear from their eyes. Death will
be no more; mourning and crying and pain will be
no more, for the first things have passed away."*
—*Revelation 21:4*

I release my deepest hurts today. No longer
will I wrestle with memories that cause me
sadness. Of course, the memories will never
go away, but the way I react to those memories will change.

It is important for me to work through the
anger, remorse, sorrow, and forgiveness in
order to put to rest the hurts that run so deep.
Today I accept my past pain, make a renewed
effort to release my deepest hurts, and go on.

When Christ comes again to claim me,
everything will be made whole. Yet even
today I can begin to put the tears, mourning,
and pain in proper perspective. Tears, and
even death, are part of life. I don't fear them,
for God is with me even when I'm in the
midst of hard times. I relax, knowing God is
in control.

**I do not fear, for God brings me comfort when
I suffer.**

---

*The Spirit and the bride say, "Come." And let every-
one who hears say, "Come." And let everyone who is
thirsty come. Let anyone who wishes take the water of
life as a gift.*   —Revelation 22:17

Today I am aware of the sense of wonder
God creates within my soul. Each day is a special miracle, and I rejoice in its new beginning. As I make a fresh start, I live in the
expectation of joy and laughter.

With eagerness I meet the Spirit who bids
me come. Filled with new hope, I drink from
the well that never runs dry. The Spirit of the
living water guides me into tomorrow.

I take inventory of my new learnings and
experiences of these past twenty-four hours.
"Did I eagerly reach out for the opportunities
presented to me and laugh with pleasure at
the wonder all around me?" If I did, then I am
taking Jesus at his word by accepting the invi-
tation to receive the gift of life-giving water,
so that I may live a hopeful and joyful life.

I continually explore God's sense of wonder.

JULY 9   *HOPE*

*"Let anyone who is thirsty come to me, and let the
one who believes in me drink. As the scripture has
said, 'Out of the believer's heart shall flow rivers of
living water.'"*   —*John 7:38*

I open my heart and mind to the water Jesus
offers this day which brings hope. In the past I
was a very thirsty person. The center of my
being was like a great desert. Without a sense
of the future, hopelessness was all I could feel.

I now know the search for living water is
not mine alone. My sisters and brothers,
neighbors, and friends all thirst for the water
that will quench their thirst for hope. In community I gain a sense of purpose and destiny.
As my colleagues and companions and I
become, in Christ, a people with a strong
sense of self-esteem, we are pulled into the
possibilities of a hope-filled future of justice,
peace, and love.

**Today I take my thirst to Jesus who gives me
hope-filled living water to drink.**

Beloved, let us love one another, because love is from God; everyone who loves is born of God and knows God.   —*1 John 4:7-8*

Today I love and have fulfilling relationships. Being born of God, I claim my freedom from lovelessness, loneliness, depression, and emptiness. I think about why I have feelings of despair in my relationships, and I face them.

As my life situation changes, it is time to re-evaluate my covenant with a loved one. Although the vows I pledged remain firm, I need to reassess and renegotiate how those vows will be lived out in everyday life. Then, perhaps, love will begin to blossom once again.

I open my mind and heart to choose the right people as companions for my journey. The words we speak to one another will convey love and mutual respect. I put effort into communication so that I build the intimacy I desire.

I claim my need to love and be loved.

JULY 11   EXPECTATION

When the LORD restored the fortunes of Zion, we were like those who dream. Then our mouth was filled with laughter, and our tongue with shouts of joy. —Psalm 126:1-2a

I find time to dream today. I consider my aspirations and goals and know that when I allow myself to dream, the dreams sometimes become realities. The pictures I draw in my own mind help to determine the realities of the future.

I brush aside the nightmares that fixated me in the past and turn my thoughts to affirming dreams. I rejoice in what I and God are accomplishing in my life because I dare to dream boldly.

As I endeavor to make my dreams a reality, barriers dissolve and constrictions disappear. Others will look at me and know that I am a person who dares to dream as well as a person who works to make those dreams come true.

With joy and laughter as my foundation, God and I are working to make my visions for the future come true.

For God alone my soul waits in silence; from him comes my salvation. He alone is my rock and my salvation, my fortress; I shall never be shaken.

—*Psalm 62:1-2*

I trust God completely. My trust in God allows me to trust myself. The biggest obstacle in my life is my fear of failure. Today I set aside this fear and do the best I can. I am not to be perfect, for only God is perfect. As long as I've tried and given it my all, even when I am unsuccessful, God does not count me a failure, and neither do I.

The better I know myself, the more I am able to be open to creative methods. As I am loved and love others, I surround myself with supportive people who want the best for me. I know and trust that the future will be filled with wondrous expressions and tremendous experiences. I continue to enjoy today and look forward with eager anticipation to tomorrow.

I trust in God who comes to me again and again.

"But those who drink of the water that I will give them will never be thirsty. The water that I will give will become in them a spring of water gushing up to eternal life." —John 4:14

Today I drink from the spring of water provided by Jesus. With my thirst quenched, I have a positive, hopeful outlook on life that moves me into the rivers of acceptance, love, and freedom.

At one time I did not drink of Christ's fountain of life. I lived as though I were in a drought and the water of life had to be rationed. My attitude was one of hopelessness, cynicism, and doubt. I moved through each day with dread and stinginess.

As I now live with abundant water coursing through me, I change my old ways of thinking and living to experience the joy of the moment. Christ's love never runs dry. Hope in Jesus is constantly bubbling up like a fountain within me, providing vital energy and spiritual strength.

As I move through this day, I drink from the eternal fountain of hope.

My vows to you I must perform, O God; I will render thank offerings to you. For you have delivered my soul from death, and my feet from falling, so that I may walk before God in the light of life.
—*Psalm 56:12-13*

Today I think the very best about myself. I do not waste time condemning myself for my inadequacies or dwelling on my failures. Instead, I invite positive expressions to be at the center of my day. I expect good things to happen, and I'm ready to greet them.

With genuine determination I set aside my negativity and clear the way for God's light to shine. I move from darkness to light. I draw people to me who are positive and promote growth. I set aside criticism and see the positive in others. I tell others how much I appreciate their positive attitude and how their hopefulness spurs me on in my own journey.

Today God is with me, leading me in positive ways.

I draw light to my life and invite positive expressions of God's leading.

JULY 15   THANKFULNESS

He was in the wilderness forty days, tempted by Satan; and he was with the wild beasts; and the angels waited on him.   —Mark 1:13

When Jesus was in the wilderness, even there he was not alone. Ministering angels surrounded him and cared for him.

Like the angels who waited on Jesus, there are ministering people who surround me this day. Friends who listen to me or hand me a tissue when I cry are like ministering angels. They've even stood by while I ranted and raved as I worked through my anger at the unfairness of life. I look back and recall individuals who sat at my bedside when I was ill, shared a cup of coffee in a time of sorrow, or cared for the nitty-gritty of life when I could only muddle through the day.

I am thankful for these people who took care of me in my need. I live humbly, knowing that I cannot make it alone through the wilderness times. I need these ministering spirits, and I am thankful for their part in my life.

I give God thanks for the people who minister to me.

The heavens proclaim his righteousness; and all the peoples behold his glory.   —Psalm 97:6

God is in heaven, and all is in order. I have a sense of belonging with God's creation—with all living things. I live respectfully with the land. If my life is chaotic and in disorder today, I look to the rain falling, the clouds rolling, and the stars shining and know I'm secure in God's presence.

Winter, spring, summer, and fall follow one after another. Snow falls, flowers bloom, crops grow, leaves turn brilliant colors, and I know all is well. Each season allows me to claim again my oneness with God and God's creation. Today I notice the beauty of the created order around me and appreciate its natural order.

I am in touch with the earth and its seasons.

JULY 17   *CHANGE*

Bless the LORD, O my soul, and do not forget all his benefits—who forgives all your iniquity, who heals all your diseases, who redeems your life from the Pit, who crowns you with steadfast love and mercy.
        —Psalm 103:2-4

Because the Lord forgives, heals, and redeems, I am able to close the book on yesterday's hurtful happenings and focus my energies on making constructive changes in my life. Equipped with a fresh beginning, I use my memories and past experiences to influence the choices I make today. I am now free to deal with the lessons of life.

I do not depend on solving all the problems of yesterday in order to proceed with my life today. Some problems are important only as they are relevant to my current situation.

God has given me a life of goodness and beauty. Yesterday is a closed book, and I'm ready to get on with today's agenda. I keep my eyes looking ahead, ready for wonderful opportunities to unfold.

Yesterday is gone, and I experience and enjoy the opportunities for change in this new day.

"Your sons and your daughters shall prophesy, and your young men shall see visions, and your old men shall dream dreams." —*Acts 2:17*b

God calls me to a new vision. My dreams inform today's struggles and tomorrow's goals. Now is the moment to look at where I've been and consider my aims and goals. There is no shame in having ideals but missing the mark. There is no disgrace in reaching for the stars but not getting there. The real tragedy lies in having no ideals, no dreams, and no stars to reach for.

With joy, I banish hopelessness from my mind. I let go of stagnating thoughts and negative choices. My dreams begin to take form today. I close the book on yesterday's doubts and focus my eyes on the potential of today.

I dare to dream, for my hope is in Christ.

Make me to know your ways, O LORD; teach me your paths. Lead me in your truth, and teach me, for you are the God of my salvation.   —Psalm 25:4-5

I have a choice today. I can drag through this day carrying past burdens, or I can put behind me past experiences that no longer define who I am and enthusiastically explore the path that God puts before me.

Today is all I have. The past is past, and the future never comes. Therefore, I value this hour by appreciating the people I encounter and the experiences I live as I seek to do God's will. If there are past experiences I need to sort out and understand, I designate specific times to deal with them.

I seek people who can help me make sense of my past. But I do not allow this exploration of the past to destroy the opportunity to do what God would have me do today. I am ready to wake up, refreshed and energized.

Today I awake to the exciting opportunities that come to those who follow Christ.

JULY 20   WHOLENESS

My mouth shall speak wisdom; the meditation of my heart shall be understanding.   —Psalm 49:3

My thoughts, feelings, and behaviors are coming together within me to create a congruent whole. There is joy in the wholeness of life. I value my feelings, listen to my thoughts, and then behave in appropriate ways.

As a child, I learned to separate my feelings and thoughts from my behavior. Now I know I can act on how I feel and what I think. My thoughts, feelings, and actions are integrated. I've opened myself to receive the rich feedback that comes when I listen, feel, and observe. As I become healthier, I seek out joyful situations where I can be the whole person I am meant to be.

I appreciate the whole person that I am becoming.

🍎

JULY 21   ACCEPTANCE

"No one sews a piece of unshrunk cloth on an old cloak, for the patch pulls away from the cloak, and a worse tear is made."   —Matthew 9:16

I know it is foolish to sew a piece of unshrunk cloth to an old article of clothing, but common sense does not provide answers to all my questions. Everything I encounter cannot be easily explained. I accept that there always will be problems inconsistent with my current understanding. So I don't waste my time racking my brain for answers that may not exist, for this exhausts me and leaves me with insufficient mental energy to resolve those issues within reach.

Today I set forth in search of solutions to the problems I can solve. Other questions will remain unanswered, and that's all right. Reality is composed of endless questions and unresolved puzzles. Today I accept the reality of the mysteries of life and marvel at the miracle of variety.

I accept that everything I encounter today doesn't have to fit my predetermined categories.

JULY 22   *CHANGE*

"When a woman is in labor, she has pain. . . . But when her child is born, she no longer remembers the anguish because of the joy. . . . So you have pain now; but I will see you again, and your hearts will rejoice."
—John 16:21-22

I've come through the valley of pain and out the other side into joy. Even in the midst of hard times I know I am at peace with myself and the world. With the pain past, I don't waste time looking back, dredging up old memories so I can feel sorry for myself. Today I have the courage to go forward in life.

Circumstances change and relationships take on new dimensions. These can be extremely difficult times unless I trust in the constancy and guidance of Jesus. Today I am at peace in the midst of change, knowing Jesus is with me each step of the way.

I leave the pain of the past behind and live joyfully with the change in my life.

"No one has greater love than this, to lay down one's life for one's friends."
                         —John 15:13

I want to enjoy satisfying relationships, and I set about today to learn how by cultivating self-observation. I note how I deal with people in ways that are fulfilling.

I surround myself with people who treat me with kindness and who care about me. I'm open to share both my good and bad times. Those whom I call friends are able to accept all of who I am. I don't have to do favors for another, put up with verbal or physical abuse, or let them put me down to find acceptance. I put my energy into friendships that offer the love and respect I require.

Today I select those I call "friend" carefully. I want healthy relationships, and I work to achieve them.

I want loving, enduring friendships, and I seek other disciples who are mature enough to want the same.

"I thank you, Father, . . . because you have hidden these things from the wise and the intelligent and have revealed them to infants." —Matthew 11:25-26

Sometimes people say to me, "You just need to make the best of the situation." But I don't feel I must make the best of every situation. Each situation has both bad and good within it. Therefore, no matter how delightful or how miserable things are, the situation is complete in itself—both bad and good. Instead of judging my life conditions as either one extreme or another, I choose to live fully in the moment, accepting it for what it offers.

At one time I measured everything by an "all or nothing" standard. Now I live in the wisdom of knowing that most of life can't be measured in extremes. I walk on the middle ground, and there I find wisdom. This path informs my decisions by telling me when I need to hold steady and be content or work for change.

I am open to the work of the Holy Spirit in my life and the life of the community in each moment.

Today my moments are informed by God's wisdom.

By the word of the LORD the heavens were made, and all their host by the breath of his mouth. He gathered the waters of the sea as in a bottle; he put the deeps in storehouses. . . . Let all the inhabitants of the world stand in awe of him.   —Psalm 33:6-8

Today I stand in awe of the Lord. My heart is enchanted with the beauty of the world. As I look at nature again, I see and appreciate its fresh splendor. I also look afresh at people I've known for years, seeing them as the persons they truly are rather than collections of my own projections and memories.

Once I did not live in God's love. I could see no beauty or possibilities. Instead, I'd already made up my mind how my day would develop. Now I marvel at each day God gives and live open to all the surprises it holds.

Today I fill my cup with love and stand in awe of God's good world.

Into your hand I commit my spirit; you have redeemed me, O LORD, faithful God. —Psalm 31:5

Today I lay out all my difficulties and problems and place my trust in God who redeems me. I let go of my denial and allow myself to face the difficult decisions for change that lay before me.

In the past I lived in denial of the needed changes. Fear created a fight-or-flight response. This was vital when I needed to protect myself from danger by providing energy for defense or escape. But when I make fear a part of everyday life, it causes dysfunctional stress and anxiety. I can no longer live this way.

I'm ready to make the needed changes, and I begin by trusting God. God wants me to be happy and whole.

In trust I commit my spirit into God's hands.

JULY 27   AUTHENTICITY

If I must boast, I will boast of the things that show my weakness. —2 Corinthians 11:30

I am able to show others how vulnerable and open I can be and thereby reveal my true self. I do not need to constantly build myself up in other people's eyes. Neither do I put myself down, acting falsely humble. I can and do share with people my frustrations, worries, joys, and passions. It helps them understand me better and not feel alone on their journey.

In the past I saw myself as a person with no choices in life. I was simply a faceless object, defenseless to the whim of everyone and everything. But that was not the real me. Now I stand up and claim my power. I make choices for myself and do not play the role of victim. Today I watch for the wounded, hurt person within me and offer myself caring love.

I know who I am, and I project my true identity.

If any are hearers of the word and not doers, they are like those who look at themselves in a mirror: for they look at themselves and, on going away, immediately forget what they were like.   —James 1:23-24

Today I see myself clearly, and I am happy to be who I am. I know my abilities and limitations and accept them. I let go of the pictures I carry of how I wish things were, and I choose reality again and again. I let go of the false self I learned to project out of fear and seek to live the reality of who I am.

I learn from each new experience in life. Even when things are falling apart, I can face up to what needs to be done. I choose to know my feelings and grow because of them. Because I take responsibility for my thoughts, fears, and behaviors. I allow myself to be who I am.

I walk through this day with a song in my heart, knowing who I am and where I am going in life.

---❦---

JULY 29   FREEDOM

*For you were called to freedom, brothers and sisters;
only do not use your freedom as an opportunity for
self-indulgence, but through love become slaves to one
another.*   —Galatians 5:13

I am a vehicle of God's freedom. I bring this
freedom to everything I do and everyone I
meet. To be a slave to others does not mean
that I allow others to abuse or mistreat me; it
means there is a mutual love and care
between us. I am unafraid of serving another
because I am filled with love.

I let go of my self-indulgent ways—my
compulsion to have more and to get more. I
use things and possessions without entering
into bondage to them. Because I am freed in
new ways, something wonderful lives in and
through me. That "something wonderful" is
Christ.

There are innumerable ways to live out the
love of Christ in my daily life, and I look for
these opportunities today.

**I am freed to be a loving person who also
receives love.**

But as for me, I walk in my integrity; redeem me, and be gracious to me. My foot stands on level ground.
           —Psalm 26:11-12a

I'm glad I'm a redeemed, gracious person full of integrity. I'm happy to be who I am, and at the same time, I listen carefully to what God and others are telling me about myself so that I may continue to grow and become the person I am meant to be.

I see through old habits that kept me tied to unempowering ways of living. These old habits include my need for approval from any man or woman, my fear of sharing my true self to anyone, and my need to correct people's impressions of me.

Today I allow others to see me as they choose, and I show myself as I truly am. I stand on level ground and am at peace with myself and other people.

As I journey on, I am thankful to be a person grounded in integrity.

"Every kingdom divided against itself becomes a desert, and house falls on house." —*Luke 11:17*

I am not divided against myself but am attuned to God's abiding wholeness within me. I manifest this wholeness in healthy relationships today. I trust myself to receive love and to handle hurt; to receive loyalty and to handle betrayal.

I trust my intuition when dealing with other people, and I listen to what my inner voice tells me about them. I acknowledge what I admire or dislike in others and recognize what is admirable in myself. I show anger and still love others. I share with others what my suspicions and doubts are, and when and how I am angry with them. I take other's anger as information and opportunity to build the relationship rather than as rejection. Finally, I tell others what my needs are and what I need from them. In all of these ways, I strive for wholeness within myself and my relationships.

Today I am free from self-defeating behavior in my relationships.

🍂

AUGUST 1 — DISCIPLESHIP

"No one after lighting a lamp puts it in a cellar, but on the lampstand so that those who enter may see the light."
—Luke 11:33

Today I'm unafraid of sharing my experience of Jesus Christ with others. Others' disbelief or ridicule cannot keep me from revealing who I am: a disciple of Jesus.

In the past I thought people who professed experiences of God were either candidates for the funny farm or religious fanatics. Now I see that I am a healthier, more balanced person because of my own faith connection to God.

I reclaim powerful rituals such as prayer and worship that feed my faith and make me strong. I focus on God's love and compassion as I discover a deeper meaning in life through my walk with Christ. As I'm in touch with God, I understand more and more the unity I have with the cosmos.

As I awaken today, I remove the mask I've worn. My fear melts away. I sing a song of joy and thanksgiving, exulting in my worthiness and connectedness as a child of God.

I'm a redeemed person, full of integrity, and I share what I've found with others.

AUGUST 2   WHOLENESS

"Your eye is the lamp of your body. If your eye is healthy, your whole body is full of light; but if it is not healthy, your body is full of darkness."

—Luke 11:34

My mind and my body are one and function together so that I can remain a healthy person. I do not fool myself by thinking that my body can be healthy if my mind is in torment.

At one time I tried to live as expected by everyone else. It seemed as if a hundred eyes were fixed on me, watching my every move and waiting for me to fail. Most of my energy went into trying to impress others. Ironically, the more I tried to control the situation, the more I fell on my face.

Now I understand and respect my mind-body connection. I take the time to reinforce relaxation responses. I promote self-awareness and make a conscious choice to re-energize myself. Seeing things clearly helps me make light-filled, healthy choices. I admit what I need to work on, and I move on.

I live in the light of Jesus.

AUGUST 3   FORGIVENESS

Be mindful of your mercy, O LORD, and of your steadfast love, for they have been from of old. Do not remember the sins of my youth or my transgressions.

—Psalm 25:6-7a

In relationships I move beyond the duality of *me* and *you* with the unity of *we*. This unity leads me to ever-deepening wisdom when lived in the way of life called forgiveness. Forgiveness is an attitude and way of living that permits me to relate to others' pain and recognize the need for compassion and love.

When I am judgmental, I focus on flaws; when I am forgiving, I focus on relational wholeness. As I learn to forgive, I become a conduit for love, peace, power, wisdom, and passion. These are life forces that lead me to a closer bond with God.

Today I experience the loving light of God, which is grace-filled and forgiving. As I forgive my own mistakes and failures, I'm also able to forgive others. I learn from the consequences of my actions as they affect other people—creating either love or fear—and I forgive.

Today I live surrounded by the forgiveness of God.

AUGUST 4   HOLINESS

Who shall ascend the hill of the LORD? And who shall stand in his holy place? Those who have clean hands and pure hearts.
                        —Psalm 24:3-4a

I glimpse "holy moments" in my day when I suddenly stand still and feel connected to God through Jesus Christ. I glimpse God in the midst of my struggles, wounds, victories, and hopes. These glimpses lead me to understanding, wisdom, and love.

I see God as one who shares in all my ups and downs, ins and outs. Mistakes are occasions for learning, and life's darkest passages are opportunities to realize love. I let go of the desire to control my destiny and understand my responsibility for living my life authentically with Christ.

I look forward with eagerness to "holy moments" between myself and God. Today I am at peace. In this moment I am quiet, and sadness and regret melt away.

I stand in "holy moments," aware of my connection to God.

You prepare a table before me in the presence of my enemies; you anoint my head with oil; my cup over-flows.
                                        —Psalm 23:5

Today I take a look at the heavy burdens I carry.

In the past, nothing I did ever seemed quite "good enough." But now I open myself to acts of grace which heal me. I look at life optimistically. I live in the simple reality of what is really important in life: *faith*, *family*, and *friends*. Today I find the courage to leave that which separates me from what I truly value.

I recognize that healing begins at home. So, no matter how many challenges I face, I leave plenty of time for my three F's. I recognize that, because of God's love for me, I am "good enough."

Healing may be a painful process because it calls me to look at my dark side and worst fears. But by grappling with darkness I eventually find light, and my pain is changed to wisdom and joy.

Today my cup overflows, even in the midst of heavy burdens.

AUGUST 6   JOY

I think of you on my bed, and meditate on you in the watches of the night; for you have been my help, and in the shadow of your wings I sing for joy.

—Psalm 63:6-7

So many times I awake in the morning anxious about the prospects of a new day. My mind replays yesterday's regrets and anticipates tomorrow's worries—even before I've climbed out of bed! This morning as I greet the world with worry and weariness, I am reminded of what I've lost with the years—the joyful state of expectation, wonder, curiosity, and gratitude in which I once delighted.

Now I reclaim those days of delight. I get up in the morning excited about the day to come. Living in the present moment, I approach life with wonder, honesty, and anticipation. I no longer cling to the security of pleasing others but am free to express my needs, moods, and desires.

I take time for myself and the people I love, dispelling the illusion that there is not enough time for my family, friends, or church. If the merry-go-round seems to be going too fast, I make the choice to slow down or step off.

I anticipate this day with joy.

AUGUST 7   FAITHFULNESS

Happy are those who do not follow the advice of the wicked, or take the path that sinners tread, or sit in the seat of scoffers; but their delight is in the law of the LORD. —Psalm 1:1-2a

Today I listen for God's presence. Sometimes I am open and hear God's voice loudly. At other times my spirit is closed, and God's voice is muffled. In all my interactions and decisions today I seek God's guidance.

I trust I'm able, guided by the Holy Spirit, to follow the straight and narrow path. Even in seasons when I am not ready or willing to listen or to be led, God continues to work in my life, sending life-giving messages. God is always with me, but so often I choose directions in opposition to what God wants for me.

Listening to God now, I am guided to serenity. I know God speaks and communicates to me in many ways. I'm open to God and know God blesses my journey today.

Today I listen to God, and I am guided in the narrow path.

AUGUST 8   *FORGIVENESS*

I lie down and sleep; I wake again, for the LORD sustains me.
— *Psalm 3:5*

As I awaken today, I forgive myself. I leave behind painful memories which no longer serve me or anyone else. My steps are lighter as I begin anew.

I need to forgive myself for the damage I've done and to build reconciliation between who I once was and who I now am. I need and seek peace, which comes when I accept my mistakes, ask God's forgiveness, and move on.

I strike from my mental tapes "If only I'd made a different decision" or "If only I'd been smarter," and I place on my tapes, "I did the best I could for the circumstances of the moment."

I am forgiving and peaceful today. This order in my life opens the door for me to be more at peace and connected in my relationships with others, God, and myself.

I awaken this morning refreshed and sustained, acknowledging those incidents that need the touch of forgiveness.

AUGUST 9   STRENGTH

"In the world you face persecution. But take courage; I have conquered the world!"

—*John 16:33b*

I claim the power granted to me as a disciple of Jesus Christ. I am provided with all the strength I need to make it through the day. As I continue to awaken to my power, I am moving and acting in bold new ways.

My life is centered in discipleship, and I know that with God's help I can handle anything thrown my way. I have the assurance that God travels with me on my journey. My walk with God undergirds my spirit and strengthens me to go in the right direction.

I throw out of my vocabulary the words "I can't" and adopt the words "I can!" I have the power to step out in faith, knowing God's power will be there when I need it.

I look to God for the power I need to meet today's challenges.

Day by day, as they spent much time together in the temple, they broke bread at home and ate their food with glad and generous hearts, praising God and having the good-will of all the people. —*Acts 2:46-47*

Today I'm grateful for all the people who have guided me and shared my joys and sorrows. Through my interactions with others I have found healing—physically, emotionally, and spiritually. We have shared our ongoing stories, struggles, and victories. Through the mutual framework of our community support, we've learned to use our love and enthusiasm to become more caring and compassionate.

In the past I was fearful of allowing anyone to come too close. Now I rejoice over the wonderful people who bless my life. They are my partners, soul mates, colleagues, and best friends. They bring a rich supply of life and a wealth of inspiration to be the best "me" I can be. Today I gratefully acknowledge these friends, realizing my life would not be as full without their presence.

I am enriched by the encouragement and insight of cherished friends.

"Go and tell John what you have seen and heard: the blind receive their sight, the lame walk, the lepers are cleansed, the deaf hear, the dead are raised, the poor have good news brought to them."   —Luke 7:22

Jesus bestowed gifts of healing and life on the people he met. Each day that he walked on the earth, Jesus was a gift to those he encountered.

Today I enjoy God's gifts, taking in the richness they offer. With my eyes wide open, I see the beauty around me. I walk and appreciate each step I take. My ears are open to listen and hear the sounds of nature. I am rich in the wonder of God's earth. I appreciate and enjoy the evidence that God's purposes and plans are being realized.

I am awake, alert, and truly alive to God's world. There is good news to be received and shared. I see myself in God's world, free from limitations. I find courage to go forward in my life, expecting good news to unfold. I make this day a new beginning.

I use God's gifts of sight, sound, and life as I live expectantly today.

AUGUST 12   TRANSFORMATION

Therefore, my beloved, be steadfast, immovable, always excelling in the work of the Lord, because you know that in the Lord your labor is not in vain.
—*1 Corinthians 15:58*

Today I continue my journey of transformation by being steadfast in my work, immovable in my pursuits, and excellent in my tasks. I follow the path as a disciple of Jesus to reach my destination.

Many times I've struggled to free myself from the chains of past inconsistencies and confusion which beckoned me in misdirected ways. Today I renew my energy and push forward. I put aside all obstacles that keep me from making needed changes in my life. I put negative thoughts on hold as I continue my commitment to growth and maturity.

Even when circumstances seem hopeless, I do not give up easily but remain steadfast in my endeavors, commitments, and responsibilities. I finish the projects I've begun and feel satisfaction in the step I've taken on my journey.

I have purpose and direction in all I undertake.

AUGUST 13　　　　COMMUNITY

If then there is any encouragement in Christ, any consolation from love, any sharing in the Spirit, any compassion and sympathy, make my joy complete: be of the same mind, having the same love, being in full accord and of one mind.　　—*Philippians 2:1-2*

I am able to love others because I have received love. I am able to share because I have experienced compassion and sympathy in my own life. I unite with my family, church, or community when a task needs to be accomplished because I have been encouraged in my own individual pursuits. I can belong to a community or group and still respect my own individuality and the individuality of others.

In times past I've tried to control friends' and relatives' behavior by continually covering up or making excuses for them. Today I know what is my responsibility and what is the responsibility of others. I am able to love people as I express God's presence through my life. In community, I share and work with others who have received Christ's encouragement and been moved by God's love.

I share God's love, and my joy is complete, as I reach out in loving ways.

"Whatever house you enter, first say, 'Peace to this house!' And if anyone is there who shares in peace, your peace will rest on that person; but if not, it will return to you."   —Luke 10:5-6

Perfect peace allows me to release all my anxiety today and live serenely with everyone I meet. At the root of my spirituality is a peace that is imperturbable. This peace allows me to live without fear and remain calm as I make sound decisions.

I feel no conflict or turmoil as I enter my home, school, or workplace. I am centered and composed as I work through each situation. I am clear about the feelings that are mine and the feelings that belong to others. Love shines from my inner peace and radiates to those around me. I wish God's best for each person I meet.

If I find I'm distracted from my peaceful ways, I call a "time out" to relax and evaluate. Anxiety disappears when I take the time to be calm and experience the peace of Christ.

In the confidence of God's peace, I live this day in harmony and serenity.

AUGUST 15   GOD'S WILL

*I thank my God every time I remember you . . .
because of your sharing in the gospel from the first
day until now. I am confident of this, that the one
who began a good work among you will bring it to
completion by the day of Jesus Christ.*

                                   —*Philippians 1:3-6*

I am not to control my loved ones or their
journeys. Jesus is at work within each of us,
and Jesus will take us where we are to be in
our journeys.

In past times I tried to take responsibility
for the actions or words of others by making
excuses for their behavior. When they shirked
responsibilities, made embarrassing blunders,
or acted in destructive ways, I apologized for
them.

Today I do not take responsibility for others' actions or conduct. I concentrate on maintaining my own personhood. I step far enough
away from them so I am not caught up in
their emotional upheaval. I learn to accept
others for who they are and allow them to be
responsible for their own lives.

**I am confident that God is uniquely at work
in each of us.**

AUGUST 16   CONFIDENCE

Do your best to present yourself to God as one approved by him, a worker who has no need to be ashamed, rightly explaining the word of truth.
—2 Timothy 2:15

I present myself to God as a confident student and teacher. I work hard and am eager to study, listen, and learn. I also enjoy sharing my understandings with others who seek to add to their knowledge. As I become more sure of my intelligence and capabilities, I am more comfortable in the roles of student and teacher.

As a child, I was afraid I would not understand a concept and be called stupid. I was shamed by adults or other children at school and at home for not "getting it right." Now I view myself as a person who can learn and retain knowledge and teach someone else what I know.

Today I embrace the opportunities to learn. I am confident of my intelligence, and I enjoy being both the student and the teacher.

I am a capable, intelligent child of God who enjoys opportunities to gain knowledge.

AUGUST 17   *LOVE*

And now faith, hope, and love abide, these three;
and the greatest of these is love.

—1 Corinthians 13:13

Love is the cornerstone of my life. I can't
have faith or hope if I do not have love. In the
past I sat on mountaintops and meditated on
lofty thoughts, forgetting to relate to people
and events around me. This is not the love the
Bible talks about.

Today I am eager to relate and interact in
loving ways with others. Isolating myself does
not permit love to flourish. Each experience I
face and every person I meet add new dimensions to the way I love. I no longer shut
myself off from people I fear. When I do this, I
only hurt myself and miss the opportunity to
love.

As I grow in love, each step I take leads me
to love more deeply. I learn to love, and I
enrich myself and those around me. My ability to love is a gift for which I'm thankful.

**I'm a person of faith and hope, but most of all,
I'm a person of love.**

You shall love the Lord your God with all your heart, and with all your soul, and with all your strength, and with all your mind; and your neighbor as yourself.
—Luke 10:27

Love of God, love of others, and love of myself are central in my life. Love is the most therapeutic and healing gift in life.

I love when I'm able to both give and receive. I love when I can both appreciate and be appreciated. I love when I act in ways that are in others' and my own best interests.

I didn't see healthy examples of love when I was growing up. Divorce was the norm in marriage, and friendships lasted only as long as they were useful.

Today I am eager and ready to love and extend myself for another. I know that couples can succeed in maintaining and growing in love over many years. Divorce does not have to be the norm, and friendships can last a lifetime.

I am a loving person, ready to love.

AUGUST 19   FRIENDSHIP

A woman named Martha welcomed him into her home. She had a sister named Mary, who sat at the Lord's feet and listened to what he was saying.
—Luke 10:38b-39

There is a bit of the personality of both Mary and Martha in me. When guests come to my home, I enjoy playing the host, sharing my hospitality. I tidy the house, ready some food, and make the visitor feel comfortable. I also relish the time spent talking over a cup of coffee, listening to stories, and learning through experiences shared.

I'm a good friend and companion. My home is a safe haven where people come to rest. My friends are able to be who they are without putting on airs or needing to perform for me. I accept who they are as individuals and tell them so. I enjoy their differences, for this is what makes our relationships fun and interesting.

My home may not be a palace, nor the food I serve gourmet, but none of that is important. What is important is my love for people and my willingness to make space for them in my life.

I'm thankful for the friends I enjoy in Jesus Christ.

"Is there anyone among you who, if your child asks for a fish, will give a snake instead of a fish? . . . If you then, who are evil, know how to give good gifts to your children, how much more will the heavenly Father give the Holy Spirit to those who ask him!"
—*Luke 11:11-13*

I am a child of God who knows how to receive good gifts. I trust God, who will not betray me or let me down.

Although my body and my intellect have grown to adulthood, I continue to live in self-protective ways because I did not receive the consistency I needed as a child. Adults told me one thing and did another. Time and time again I was disappointed, until I no longer counted on anyone for anything.

My chaotic childhood is now a memory. As a parent, I live differently with my children. I don't make promises I can't keep. They know I am a person of my word. I give them the consistent discipline and love I missed in my own childhood.

Today I am a trustworthy parent to my children.

"Ask, and it will be given you; search, and you will find; knock, and the door will be opened for you."
—Luke 11:9

I ask, I search, and I knock. I know I do not leave empty-handed, but that the harvest will be bountiful.

First, I ask. To ask means that I value myself and know I am worthy of what I'm asking for. I view my thoughts, feelings, and desires as important, and I ask for what I want and need.

Second, I search, not only for answers from the wisdom of God but also from the wisdom I have within. My inner strength allowed me to survive this far, and it will not fail me now. Finally, I knock—loudly and with force. At this moment I recognize that God wants my life to be full and abundant.

Today I do not sit idly by, waiting for what I need to drop in my lap, but I take action. Jesus assures me that as I ask, search, and knock, the door will be opened and I will find what I need.

In a life grounded in prayer, I *ask* to receive, *search* to find, and *knock* to have the door opened.

"I tell you that many prophets and kings desired to see what you see, but did not see it, and to hear what you hear, but did not hear it." —Luke 10:24

I possess wisdom which directs me in my day-to-day living. I'm in touch with the person I am becoming in Christ, because I take the time to pray, to see, and to hear. My eyes are wide open and my ears are alert as I claim the power to live with strength and passion.

How do I know when I'm seeing and hearing with wisdom? I know—when I don't have to do everything perfectly. I know—when I realize that every relationship that fails is not my fault. I know—when I see the reality of the situation and continue to live in hope. I know—when I'm proud of being myself.

These signs, seeing and hearing with wisdom, grow gradually, through time and discipline. When I notice the changes, then I know my struggles are worth the effort.

I am a wise person, with my eyes wide open and my ears tuned.

But the Lord answered her, "Martha, Martha, you are worried and distracted by many things; there is need of only one thing. Mary has chosen the better part, which will not be taken away from her."
—Luke 10:41-42

Martha thought her sister, Mary, was not making the right choice. Mary chose to sit and learn from Jesus, but Martha thought she should be doing the "womanly" things expected by society. Mary held fast to what she knew was right for her, and Jesus supported her actions.

Today I choose to do what is right for me. I no longer allow my family to dictate what is expected. I know who I am and where God is leading me, and I live my life with certainty. I refuse to feel guilty or ashamed for taking care of my needs.

I'm freed today from choices that are not for my good. The patterns I now follow are satisfying and fulfilling. I'm learning to care for myself and to find new ways to make sound choices.

Like Mary, I choose what is right for me.

"No one who puts a hand to the plow and looks back is fit for the kingdom of God." —Luke 9:62

This day, and every day hereafter, I hold before me the vision of who I am becoming. In this moment I reflect on my chosen direction. I see a dream of what my life can become as I pursue the work that will make my dream a reality.

Like a farmer, I step away from time to time to evaluate the whole field—the work done and the work left to do. I then move onward to continue my plowing. I rejoice in the person I am today, turn to my chosen work, and do the best I can.

Seeing the wonderful opportunities for growth that lie ahead, I move on. I strive forward as a capable adult. As I develop the picture of my life, I have a sense of growing competence.

Today I look toward the future expectantly.

AUGUST 25 *HUMILITY*

"Whoever welcomes this child in my name welcomes me, and whoever welcomes me welcomes the one who sent me; for the least among all of you is the greatest."
—Luke 9:48

Jesus tells me that becoming like a child in some ways is good. I'm to turn away from self-chosen goals and relate to God as a child relates to a beloved parent. I am to demonstrate child-*like* relations, not child*ish* behavior.

Today I take responsibility for my behavior. This means I think before I act. It means I'm at home in who I am and where I belong in life, and I don't need to squabble about it with others. I am self-assured and centered in Christ. I'm able to serve others because I don't need to prove myself to them or to anyone else.

Ambition is good when I want to make a difference in the world with my life. I need ambition and drive to get where I feel called to go. But when my ambition causes me to put others down or compete in selfish ways, it serves no one, least of all myself. I don't need to be the "important one," because I am good enough to my heavenly parent and to myself.

Today I reclaim the child within me who is self-assured and does not worry about being important in other people's eyes.

AUGUST 26   THANKFULNESS

*Sing praises to the LORD, O you his faithful ones,
and give thanks to his holy name.*   —Psalm 30:4

Saying yes and participating in life require my immediate and complete attention. When I'm aware and attentively present, I experience peace, wisdom, and compassion.

As I awaken from my calm night's sleep, I do not immediately begin to rumble and whirl with worry and concern. Instead, I say my morning prayers, asking for God's blessing, and calmly look forward to the new day.

Today I am thankful for cherished moments —moments spent laughing with loved ones, hugging someone I care for, or walking in the brisk fresh air. These are moments when I'm in touch with myself, with others, and with God. As I enjoy these "holy moments" alone and in the company of others, I sense there is a three-way bridge linking me with others and with God.

Today I give thanks as I experience the day fully.

Answer me when I call, O God of my right! You gave me room when I was in distress. Be gracious to me, and hear my prayer. . . . But know that the LORD has set apart the faithful for himself; the LORD hears when I call to him. —Psalm 4:1, 3

Today I quiet myself before God and direct my mind through prayer. This helps me perform my actions in the world more competently, lovingly, honestly, and confidently. Prayer is truly a gift, for it helps me to sort out life's complications, and it strengthens my connection to God.

I take an open attitude toward prayer. I do not worry if my mind wanders at times, nor do I worry about the quality of my prayers. I simply pray, assured that my time is well spent.

I close my eyes, take a few deep breaths, and pray.

O LORD my God, I cried to you for help, and you have healed me. —Psalm 30:2

I have lived through the "dark night of my soul." In the midst of my hopelessness I cried to God for help, and God heard me. I told God of my sorrow and desolation, and God healed me.

Now the dark night of my soul is passing, and the light of day leads me. Today I am joyful as God heals my brokenness and puts the fragmented pieces of my heart back together.

Each day I find new strength and learn new ways to live through difficult circumstances. I take care of myself and my needs. I nourish my soul so that I may be whole.

When I step back and conduct an inventory of my journey, I am amazed by how far I've come. I am assured that no problem will last forever. I bear the pain I encounter today, knowing tomorrow will bring resolve. I rejoice, even as I continue to heal.

I travel into the healing light, assured that God is with me.

But by the grace of God I am what I am, and his grace toward me has not been in vain.

—*1 Corinthians 15:10*a

Today I experience and accept God's grace. Grace, unsought and unearned, blows through my life, and all I need to do is raise my sails to take full advantage.

In the past I was unable to live in God's grace. I placed my hope of salvation in engaging the pity of the oppressor, so that I might feel enraged at my ill treatment. In this way I compensated for the helplessness and fear I felt.

I now step out of this self-defeating pattern. Of course, old patterns die hard. But I look for opportunities to practice being aware of my conditioned reactions, and I make new choices. Some days I succeed, and some days I don't. I let God know that I need help. I no longer feel like a hopeless child but a beloved, grace-filled child of God.

Today I open my sails to catch the full wind of God's grace.

⚜

AUGUST 30   HEALING

*As a deer longs for flowing streams, so my soul longs
for you, O God.*   —Psalm 42:1

Am I afraid to long for God and open myself
to all the possibilities God has for my life? Do
I still block God's work within me by denying
my emotions and feelings? To feel takes courage, but when I do not feel, I cut myself off
from the joy—as well as the pain—of life.

I no longer cut myself off from the pain and
pleasure of life. I am awake, and I learn from
all my experiences. I allow my emotions to
enrich my spiritual journey. My emotions are
an important resource that brings healing.

**Today I quench my thirst with the living water
of feelings and emotions.**

AUGUST 31   HOPE

I am bringing you good news of great joy for all the people: to you is born this day in the city of David a Savior, who is the Messiah, the LORD.

—*Luke 2:10b-11*

There is good news to tell and to receive, and this brings me hope. As I arise this morning, I see the world as never before. Today there is joy in my step.

At one time in my life I felt as if I were sleepwalking through each day. Now, perhaps for the first time, I feel alive. I feel the aliveness that comes from Christ, and I know I never will be content to sleepwalk again.

Today I add new phrases to my vocabulary —words such as "I am," "I need," and "I feel." With hope for tomorrow, I leap into the dawn of my new life.

Today I hear and tell the good news of hope.

SEPTEMBER 1   *PRAYER*

And after he had dismissed the crowds, he went up the mountain by himself to pray. When evening came, he was there alone. —Matthew 14:23

In order to think and pray, I find time apart from the normal activities of my day. I know that relationships play an important part in my life, but they do not define me entirely. I recognize my autonomy and therefore do not cling to dependent relationships to fill my empty spaces.

I have a community of people who give me support, comfort, and assistance as I need it, but I know there is work that only I can do. My life of thoughtful prayer can be done only by me. If I'm to foster my own growth, I need moments alone for reflection. I meet these times of aloneness with peaceful expectation.

Today I take the time I need for thought and prayer.

SEPTEMBER 2   RELATIONSHIPS

"For where two or three are gathered in my name, I am there among them."   —Matthew 18:20

I'm part of a healthy community, and I am able to select relationships that are good for me. As my self-image improves, I choose to spend time with people who feel good about themselves and about me.

No longer do I gravitate toward people who are unbalanced, addicted, or disrespectful of themselves or of me. I'm not infatuated by people who mistreat themselves and other people. Getting bogged down in unstable relationships takes too much energy that can be used in more creative ways. If I sense myself being pulled toward self-defeating relationships, I recognize it and pull back.

I need women and men in my life who are stable and treat me with respect. I need a community of Christian people who are healthy and balanced. The added gift is that Jesus will be present with us.

As I grow in my own health, I attract healthy relationships.

SEPTEMBER 3   SELF-ACCEPTANCE

"If a shepherd has a hundred sheep, and one of them has gone astray, does he not leave the ninety-nine on the mountains and go in search of the one that went astray? And if he finds it, truly I tell you, he rejoices over it more than over the ninety-nine that never went astray."   —Matthew 18:12b-13

I rejoice in knowing I'm an important member of God's family. I may be one of the ninety-nine, or I may be the one gone astray. Whatever the case, I am of value to the shepherd.

At one time I felt like a throwaway. I believed that if I wandered away, like the lost sheep, no one would come in search of me, and I'd be lost. Now I know that I am important. I'm important to God and to the people who love me, and I'm extremely important to myself. I no longer have to prove how valuable I am by working myself to death. Being a martyr will not win the end I seek.

Today I give myself permission to value ME. I also invite those who love me to tell me how I'm important in their lives. I take it all in and recognize how good it feels.

I'm thankful that Jesus values my life.

I cry aloud to God, aloud to God, that he may hear me. In the day of my trouble I seek the LORD.

—Psalm 77:1-2a

The future is hopeful. There are innumerable possibilities for growth and fulfilling relationships. Seeing all these opportunities lets me know that I'm not trapped but have many choices.

I'm no longer a helpless victim stuck in a futile environment. Now I am a competent, capable adult, ready to meet the challenges ahead with enthusiasm and confidence. I look to the future with a growing sense of excitement.

When I take time to step back and survey my life situation, the problems I have seem manageable. There is nothing I will encounter today that, with God's help, I cannot handle. If I experience difficulties, I know they won't last forever.

In whatever happens today, I remain calm and assured, reminding myself that God is with me.

I seek God, especially in times of difficulty, and I'm not disappointed.

SEPTEMBER 5   *LOVE*

"Love your neighbor as yourself." —Matthew 22:39

I respect and love others just as I respect and love myself. Because my self-esteem is secure, I can esteem others equally. This love for myself and others overflows from the love I have from God, who names us acceptable. There is mutuality in my relationships.

I have no doubts about my worth, and I am not at the mercy of the approval of others. I do not interpret questionable incidents as evidence that I'm being rejected because I am not acceptable or lovable. I recognize that other people's actions may simply stem from preoccupation with issues that do not involve me. The world does not revolve around me.

I am secure in God's love as I extend love to others, just as I give it to myself.

Because of God's reciprocal love, I am able to love others.

SEPTEMBER 6   HAPPINESS

*Your steadfast love, O LORD, extends to the heavens,
your faithfulness to the clouds.*   —Psalm 36:5

I find happiness on the path I've chosen and feel content and fulfilled. I am secure in God's steadfast love and faithfulness.

There are forks in the road where the choices I make determine if I am to be happy or unhappy. To be happy, I may need to separate myself emotionally from family members. I am learning that I cannot appease my parents or siblings at the expense of my own happiness, or sacrifice my own well-being in order to play the role of family protector or savior. Neither do I continue to chase after "fire engines," stirring up tension and conflict in my relationships.

If I am happy today, it is because I've learned how to find happiness and contentment in my own way. I grow in strength and self-discovery as I live in God's faithfulness and steadfast love. I choose the path of happiness.

Whatever situation comes my way, I remain content and happy, centered in God's love.

"Have you not read that . . . 'a man shall leave his father and mother and be joined to his wife, and the two shall become one flesh'? So they are no longer two, but one flesh."
— Matthew 19:4a, 5-6a

I choose to see my relationships as they really are. I enter into relationships, knowing that no one can care for all my needs.

A past fantasy was that a knight in shining armor or a perfect princess would sweep into my life and solve all my problems. I expected the relationship to heal all my wounds and resolve all my issues.

Now I enter my relationships realistically. I respect the other person as he or she is, and I expect this person to respect me. I do not melt into the other person, losing my identity. Neither do I expect this person to deny who he or she is and become like me. Instead, we join in partnership to complement and support each other. I do not give up my individuality but use who I am as an individual to enhance the relationship.

I see myself and the other person for who we are.

"Unless you change and become like children, you will never enter the kingdom of heaven."
—Matthew 18:3

Children are honest people. They are clear in the communication of their needs. Yet somewhere along the way they learn to stop communicating openly and to repress their desires. In order to survive, they disown their own feelings.

Today I recapture childlike honesty. I clear the air and employ honest, open communication. I challenge the denial of my feelings of happiness, anger, joy, and sadness. I no longer put a smile on my face while crying inside. To be alienated from my feelings is disastrous for me. I am honest, and I admit my feelings to myself. In this way I begin to work for resolution.

I am free and willing to experience my emotions.

SEPTEMBER 9   ACCEPTANCE

"Let the little children come to me, and do not stop them; for it is to such as these that the kingdom of heaven belongs."   —Matthew 19:14

The greatest gift a person can give to another is the gift of acceptance. To unconditionally accept someone is a gift of love.

I often desire to have someone who will listen to me and take me seriously. I don't want to be told what to do. I seek those who will be available to me. With them I can express myself without feeling that each word I say must be brilliant or build toward some end result.

I surround myself with people who are disciples of Jesus. I seek friends who give me the time I need and accept me for who I am. I also listen respectfully to other people, knowing that they, too, are children of God's family and are loved by Jesus.

I am surrounded by friends who accept, value, and listen to one another.

"Come to me, all you that are weary and are carry-ing heavy burdens, and I will give you rest. Take my yoke upon you, and learn from me; for I am gentle and humble in heart, and you will find rest for your souls."
                                        —Matthew 11:28-29

I seek and find rest for my soul. When I grow weary of the difficulties of life and feel my burdens are too heavy for me to go on, I know I can turn to Jesus, who will give me the rest and assurance I need. I am in touch with what I need to make it through the day. My soul's desires matter, and I am not afraid to express what I want.

As a child, I thought I had to do it all by myself, keeping my worries inside. I feared that if I disclosed myself to others, they would not respond—or, worse, they would say no.

Today I take the risk, realizing what I need and asking for it. The response may be differ-ent from what I expect, but the price is too high when I don't ask. In prayer I take the opportunity to discover and ask for what I need to lighten my burden, ease my weari-ness, and find rest.

My mind is at rest, knowing I have a Savior who gently eases my burdens.

"And even the hairs of your head are all counted. So do not be afraid; you are of more value than many sparrows."   —Matthew 10:30-31

God values all of who I am! I celebrate my sexuality and acknowledge myself as a sexual person. My celebration is a tribute to myself and the person with whom I have chosen to share my life. I equate sex with care, love, and respect.

I no longer accept old myths about sex and myself as a sexual person. I know that sex is not for one person to wield power over another. Nor is sex what validates me as a man or a woman. If I was taught that sex is "dirty," I now know this is untrue.

With a new attitude, I'm now in tune with my sexual feelings. I no longer pretend my body does not exist. Sexuality is part of who I am as a total person and a disciple of Jesus.

My sexuality is a part of who I am, and I celebrate its value.

SEPTEMBER 12   COMMUNITY

Taking the five loaves and two fish, he looked up to heaven, and blessed and broke the loaves, and gave them to the disciples, and the disciples gave them to the crowds. And all ate and were filled.
—Matthew 14:19b-20a

Today I eat and am filled. I am nourished, perhaps not by bread and fish but by the knowledge that Jesus is with me, blessing me on my journey. I am blessed when I enter into intimate relationships with realistic expectations. I am blessed when I respect my own integrity and growth process. I am blessed when I recognize that my feelings, thoughts, and desires are important and valid.

I am especially blessed with a community that surrounds me and gives me support. Being nurtured means creating a flourishing environment for myself and others that promotes healthy, Christ-centered living. If I am not participating in a Christian community that aids me in my walk of discipleship, I now consciously seek one. This meal is one I cannot eat alone. Jesus does not intend for me to make it alone.

On my pathway to self-discovery, I join with others to be blessed and nurtured.

SEPTEMBER 13   HAPPINESS

Clap your hands, all you peoples; shout to God with loud songs of joy.
          —Psalm 47:1

Today I give myself permission to feel great! I clap my hands and shout for joy because I am freer, stronger, and happier than I've ever been before. Although I consider feedback from friends, relatives, and associates, I do not turn to them for approval of my well-being. All the approval I need to be happy comes from God.

Today I am not critical of myself. I set aside old voices that tell me I'm not good enough. Sometimes my interpretations of circumstances are invalid because of faulty triggers that lead to faulty perceptions. I must be on my guard to recognize these misperceptions which only undermine my happiness and contentment.

Today I give myself permission to explore all the joys of life. I willingly enter into experiences and activities that will bring me happiness.

I clap, shout, and sing because God is with me and I am strong, happy, and free.

SEPTEMBER 14 HAPPINESS

*O taste and see that the LORD is good; happy are
those who take refuge in him.* —Psalm 34:8

I taste and see that life in Jesus is good. I am
positive and happy as I seek wholeness in my
life. Today I observe the entire banquet of life.

As I strive to be happy and content, I realize
that preparing one dish does not necessarily
equate with having the whole table in order.
In other words, treating one symptom does
not heal all of who I am or take care of all my
problems. Today I take inventory of all my
symptoms so I can understand the big picture
and make needed changes.

I am a complete person—the sum of all the
dishes served at a banquet. As I strive for completeness, I examine all of who I am with gentleness and honesty. This loving observation
puts me on the road to happiness.

**As I taste all of life and see myself as I truly
am, I make needed changes so I can be happy.**

You desire truth in the inward being; therefore teach me wisdom in my secret heart.   —Psalm 51:6

Today I begin my search for hope-filled solutions. I realize there are no pat answers to my problems, and I do not expect them. Neither do I circle around my problems, worrying relentlessly. This type of worry only leaves me tired and anxious. It takes both my spiritual and my mental energy and leaves me empty.

Today I ask God for truth in my inward being. I ask God to teach me wisdom in areas of my heart that I have hidden even from myself. I begin by changing my attitude. I open my heart and mind to new ways of thinking and being. My journey of discipleship has only just begun, and the best is yet to come.

Today I desire truth in my inward being, and I ask God to teach me wisdom in my secret heart.

"For what will it profit them if they gain the whole world but forfeit their life?" —Matthew 16:26a

I remind myself that I forfeit my life when I try to control all that happens to and around me. I remind myself that life is not a constant problem to be solved but a wondrous mystery waiting to unfold. Enjoying the mystery of life rather than needing to control all that happens is important. Today I look for opportunities to live life in freeing ways.

In the past I believed I could control my family and other people, and I tried to keep a tight grip on the reins. I now realize I've been unrealistic about what I can and cannot do.

Today I resolve to look for ways to release control. I look for safe, supportive opportunities in which I can experiment in "letting go." I move slowly as I test out the waters and learn how it feels to be freed from the consuming need to control everything and everybody.

Starting today, I release my tight grip on my life and allow God to take control.

SEPTEMBER 17   HONESTY

Lord, let our eyes be opened.   —*Matthew 20:33*

I live today with my eyes wide open. This new life is mine because I've confronted my past with honesty and am now moving through transformation to a new discovery of myself and God.

At one time I lived with unrealistic expectations. I believed that if my dreams were fulfilled, I'd no longer have any problems. Now I see these "rescue fantasies" for what they are: dreams of unreality and grandiosity. I now know that even when I do realize a dream, I still must go back to living my daily life with all its assets and limitations.

Now I see the disparity between expectations and reality. I see each situation for what it is. I not only notice the improvements, but I also notice the things that remain unchanged.

As a disciple of Jesus I have regained my sight, and my eyes are open to face this day realistically.

"Do you believe that I am able to do this?" They said to him, "Yes, Lord." Then he touched their eyes and said, "According to your faith let it be done to you." And their eyes were opened. —Matthew 9:28b-30a

Because I have faith in the one who can heal, I no longer need to live in the dark despair of fear and depression. If this means I must leave a living or working condition that's destructive to my health, I am able to do so.

I no longer believe God wants me to live in darkness. I do not believe that God wants to punish me; rather, I know I get well as I acknowledge God's expressed love. My healing is in Jesus' expression of God's best wishes and richest blessings for me.

Whenever I am immobilized by fear or depression, I remember my past blindness as a remnant of the destructive conditions under which I once lived. Now I shun yesterday's painful experiences and move on. I make daily choices to avoid the darkness of the past that drew me into self-defeating patterns. I base my life on a firm faith in Jesus Christ.

In faith I say "Yes, Lord!" to life, and, according to my faith, I am healed.

SEPTEMBER 19   HOLINESS

Pursue peace with everyone, and the holiness without which no one will see the Lord.   *—Hebrews 12:14*

God calls me to be a person who is peaceful and holy. I am a person who is holy in heart and life. This means I seek to live a life of justice, mercy, truth, and, most of all, love. My holiness is cultivated by my spiritual disciplines and my life of service. Grounded in my faith in God's grace, I live my life daily in works of love and service to others.

The real challenge for me is to sustain this holiness and love in my daily life. To live faithfully each day, I seek others who also want to live a holy life. Together we help one another to be holy and loving and to express God's universal love in our daily lives.

Today I open myself to God's presence in my life and the divine witness through me to my present world.

SEPTEMBER 20   CHANGE

Neither death, nor life, nor angels, nor rulers, nor things present, nor things to come . . . nor anything else in all creation, will be able to separate us from the love of God in Christ Jesus our Lord.
—*Romans 8:38-39*

Change is difficult, and sometimes change hurts. But even as my own life shifts and the world around me moves faster, I am able to face the challenges and make the necessary adjustments. When change comes, I am able to respond in appropriate ways and deal with the ramifications.

In the past I resisted any kind of change— even change that would be positive. I became virtually paralyzed by the fear of the unknown. It was easier to stick with the status quo than to try something new. It was difficult to give up predictable ways, patterns, and modes of functioning.

Now I handle change as it comes my way. I can even handle the occasional "wipe-out" in an intelligent, informed, and thoughtful way Today I weather the changes and land on my feet.

Even in the midst of change, I stand firm and am energized for action.

SEPTEMBER 21   CHANGE

*Call on me in the day of trouble; I will deliver you,
and you shall glorify me.*   —Psalm 50:15

How do I handle myself when in the midst
of trouble and change? Do I stand rigidly
against the breakers, only to be flung down on
the shore? Or can I allow myself to ride the
waves, go with the unpredictable surf, and
land safely on shore? The choice is mine.

Today I avoid self-defeating traps and open
my eyes to see situations realistically. As I
make changes in my life, I set reasonable
goals. Trying to make big changes overnight
leads to procrastination and discouragement.
Making smaller, concrete, obtainable changes
helps me keep my goal in sight.

I send myself positive messages today: "I
can meet the challenge and do a fine job!" "I
can live through this day of trouble, go with
the flow, and deal with whatever comes my
way!"

**I meet change with assertiveness, knowing
God will deliver me.**

SEPTEMBER 22   EVANGELISM

"The harvest is plentiful, but the laborers are few; therefore ask the Lord of the harvest to send out laborers into his harvest." —Matthew 9:37-38

Jesus told his disciples to go out and gather in the overflowing harvest. I have worked long and hard throughout the year, and it is now time for me to gather in what I've toiled over.

I attend to the harvest in my own life. If I've planted seeds and attended to my crops, I will have an abundant supply in the harvest. But if I have not given myself the time needed to cultivate and nurture my seeds, I will glean little from the fields. To reap the abundant life Jesus promised, I must be certain I am making conscious choices that will give me the return I plan for and desire. If I am busy running around, spreading seed here and there and not intentionally cultivating any of my plantings, my harvest will be negligible.

Jesus invites others to join in the harvest that is plentiful for those who are willing to be laborers in the fields.

I am a willing laborer, and I accept Jesus' call to join with others in reaping a plentiful harvest.

SEPTEMBER 23 TRANSITION

God is our refuge and strength, a very present help in trouble. Therefore we will not fear, though the earth should change, though the mountains shake in the heart of the sea. —Psalm 46:1-2

Today I face the changes I need to make in my life. I expect all significant transitions to lead me to new self-discovery, yet even changes for the better are stressful. I have only a certain amount of energy to deal with the stress of change. Therefore, I weigh my options carefully so I will not burn out.

One way I minimize overload is to cut back on activities and obligations, even ones I enjoy. I weigh carefully what is most important to continue and what can be set aside, at least for this time of stress. I also consider the people in my life who are helpful in times of change and those I should not include in my life right now.

Today I do not fear the unknown, nor am I threatened by the new. I give up old ways that no longer work and try something new. I take responsibility for the changes I make.

I know that God is my refuge and strength when my world is in upheaval.

SEPTEMBER 24   COURAGE

Jesus spoke to them and said, "Take heart, it is I; do not be afraid." —Matthew 14:27

It takes courage to live in a fully conscious state, rather than to live on "automatic." To cope with the world, I must be aware of every action I take, and this can be excruciating!

Unconsciousness is even more painful, especially when I must handle unwanted or unexpected change. Yet I know that most things that happen to me do not come without warning. I no longer hold the fantasy that I am a victim, but I accept the responsibility that is mine by recognizing the warning signals. Jesus gives me the courage to recognize these signals and to make wise decisions as I am faced with change. Sometimes I soften a blow that I know is coming by developing new skills and expertise or by expanding my networks into new areas.

Today I have the courage to live in realistic, conscious ways, and I am happier for it. I no longer am my own worst enemy but my own best friend.

With Jesus beside me I am not afraid to live this day conscious of my responsibilities and opportunities.

SEPTEMBER 25   STRENGTH

Jesus came and touched them, saying, "Get up and do not be afraid." —Matthew 17:7

Today I get up, and I am not afraid. Because Jesus has touched me, I have inner strength to live my life in new ways. I am a survivor who no longer will experience life as something that happens *to* me. I have choices and rights, and I assert myself and claim what is mine. No longer will I sit around sharing "isn't it terrible" stories. Neither will I put myself in situations where I have no choice. I empower other people to move in positive ways without giving away my own power.

If I've been hurt, I take action to do something about it. If I've hurt someone else, I take action to make amends. Today and every day I claim my inner strength to make choices in my daily life.

I am strengthened because Jesus touches me.

SEPTEMBER 26 FAITH

"For truly I tell you, if you have faith the size of a mustard seed, you will say to this mountain, 'Move from here to there,' and it will move; and nothing will be impossible for you." —Matthew 17:20b-21

Today I have the faith to set my goals without fear. I choose the mountains needing change, and I work to move them. As I pursue happiness and wholeness, I declare I will succeed. I no longer sabotage myself in ways that cause my defeat, but I accept and affirm the good feelings that spring from my successes.

Sometimes living in unacceptable conditions seems easier than going through the trauma and uncertainty of change. Although I've learned from the difficult, troubling times of the past, I know that suffering in itself has no value. Now I do not waste time and energy pursuing a life that can never be fulfilling or happy. Faith in Christ enables me to move mountains, piece by piece.

Today, in faith, I set and pursue goals without fear.

"The kingdom of heaven is like treasure hidden in a field, which someone found and hid; then in his joy he goes and sells all that he has and buys that field."
—Matthew 13:44

Today I find and claim the treasure that is mine. I am ready to exchange all that I have for the truth that I have found.

I realize that something in my life was not working. I was holding myself captive with assumptions that I now know never worked. As I grow in my awareness of these false assumptions, they become a catalyst for change.

Now that I have seen my treasures once hidden, I can no longer go back or accept anything less. I welcome new opportunities and enjoy the miraculous possibilities that this new discovery brings.

I exchange my old ways for newfound treasures of truth.

———— ❧ ————

SEPTEMBER 28   CHANGE

"Be still and know that I am God!"   —*Psalm 46:10*

Today I take the first step in initiating change in my life, and I trust God with the outcome. Discipline in Christ is a motivating force in my life. Life-giving change is strategic to my growth.

I once dreaded change. There were so many upheavals that brought uncertainty and insecurity in my life. I sought comfort in routine and unchanging surroundings. I shied away from new people and events.

Now I welcome change and comfortably invite new people and challenges to confront me. When new circumstances come, I remain still, peaceful, and at ease. I don't panic but proceed in my thoughts and actions calmly. Through Christ I am empowered to live day by day.

In stillness I pray and come to understand what is best. God guides me in my decisions, and when I am ready, I move to action.

I am still and know that God is in control.

"Again, the kingdom of heaven is like a merchant in search of fine pearls; on finding one pearl of great value, he went and sold all that he had and bought it."   *—Matthew 13:45*

Today is the day! I have been searching for a long time, and now I am ready to take action. The time for me to make a decision about change in my life has arrived. I seek the support and help I need and step out in faith.

I don't wait to do something about my employment situation, my family problems, or my troubled relationships. I know what I need, and I do what I must do to take care of myself.

If there are other people involved, such as children, I realize they need help, too. I wait no longer for the help that I and they need. The time is right; the moment is now!

Today it's time to claim my pearl!

"The reason I speak to them in parables is that 'seeing they do not perceive, and hearing they do not listen, nor do they understand.'. . . But blessed are your eyes, for they see, and your ears, for they hear."

—*Matthew 13:13, 16*

Today my eyes are wide open and my ears are alert to the universe around me. I let go of rigidity and go with the flow of the day. I do not panic or become confused, but I marvel at the miracle of reality. I accept that I am not perfect and that I live in an imperfect world. Because I am human, I can accept my imperfections. Neither do I demand that others be perfect. I feel free when I see reality in this way.

There is no room for recrimination and false guilt over my lack of perfection. I do the best I can in each circumstance, and I am less demanding of myself and others as I realize that nothing in life is perfect.

I perceive, listen, and understand to the fullest extent possible, leaving perfection to God.

If we say that we have no sin, we deceive ourselves, and the truth is not in us. If we confess our sins, he who is faithful and just will forgive us our sins and cleanse us from all unrighteousness. —1 John 1:8-9

Growth as a disciple of Jesus Christ means becoming more honest with myself. I am cultivating honesty in both my words and actions. Denial has no place in my new life.

I admit my sins and work to resolve them. I face my problems willingly, and by this I am strengthened in my resolve to live as an honest person. When I admit my sins and problems, I grow in my awareness of what needs to be changed. But when I deny and cover up my problems—thinking that I won't have to deal with them if I don't admit them—these monsters only grow larger and more powerful, taking on a life of their own.

No longer will I deceive myself by saying I have no sin. Instead, I face what needs to be faced and live feeling both forgiven and clean.

I no longer carry the grime and dirt of my sins, because I am forgiven.

OCTOBER 2   DISCERNMENT

How does God's love abide in anyone who has the world's goods and sees a brother or sister in need and yet refuses help?   —1 John 3:17

It's important that what I say matches what I do. I will work to assure that my actions and words are at one with each other.

Growing up I observed adults making empty promises. Adults tried to manipulate me with wonderful words that meant nothing. Even now, as an adult, I sometimes am attracted to people who make grandiose promises but never follow through. Perhaps I want to believe so badly that I fail to notice when promised actions never come.

On this day I resolve to discern whether or not people's words and actions match. Whether they be relatives, friends, or ambitious politicians, I hold all accountable to do what they say they will do. I will not be fooled.

I know that God's love abides within me when my words and actions are congruent.

OCTOBER 3   SPIRITUAL HEALTH

*Build yourselves up on your most holy faith; pray in
the Holy Spirit; keep yourselves in the love of God.*
—Jude 1:20b-21a

My spiritual health is dependent upon my
devotion to study, meditation, and prayer.
Today I avail myself to these disciplines and
observe how much better I feel afterwards.

I've spent much of my time and energy
serving those in need, listening and giving
counsel to friends in distress, and reaching out
to those experiencing difficult circumstances.
These acts of kindness are worthy of my time
and energy, but when they are not balanced
with time spent in spiritual reflection and
renewal I become drained, burnt out, dis-
traught, and even depressed.

In the past I believed that doubling up on
my work load was commendable, and I
wanted people to know what a hard worker I
was. I no longer need to prove my worth to
myself or others. Instead, I nurture my soul
which leads to happiness, peace, and joy.

**Today I give myself permission to take time
out to care for my spiritual self.**

OCTOBER 4   STRENGTH

*You are strong and the word of God abides in you,
and you have overcome the evil one.* —*1 John 2:14*b

I base this day on the firm belief that I am
overcoming the "evil one" and growing
stronger each hour. My life is changing as I
overcome my fear and seek joyful situations.
As I grow stronger, I find that I no longer want
to live in fear, despair, and indecision. I
acknowledge God's love and presence in my
life with each newly gained strength. My new-
found wholeness is an expression of my
Christ-centered life.

When necessary, I can walk away from situations that would pull me down. No longer do
I believe that I must suffer through unchange-
able situations or that God is ready to punish
me at any moment. These are leftover beliefs
from a previous time that have no place in my
new understanding.

I make strong choices today, avoiding beliefs or feelings that throw me back into self-
defeating patterns. My life is founded on the
happiness that comes from living as a disciple.

**I am becoming stronger because I live in
God's ways.**

Let us therefore approach the throne of grace with boldness, so that we may receive mercy and find grace to help in time of need. —Hebrews 4:16

I live my life with boldness, making the best decisions I can throughout my day. I realize I will make mistakes and later admit that a different course might have been better. But I do not focus my energies on each small thing I have done wrong or might have done differently. I recognize that I am human and that only God is perfect.

I release irrational guilt and meticulous perfectionism and, therefore, make steady gains in my spiritual well-being. I am at ease as I make choices today. No longer am I trapped in destructive behavior that dissects every action I take.

I seek God's mercy and grace with the same boldness I use to make decisions and act. Always I acknowledge God's presence in my life and celebrate my humanity.

Grace and mercy are mine as I live today in bold new ways.

OCTOBER 6   RELATIONSHIPS

You must make every effort to support your faith with goodness, and goodness with knowledge, and knowledge with self-control, and self-control with endurance, and endurance with godliness, and godliness with mutual affection, and mutual affection with love.
—2 Peter 1:5-7

Faith, goodness, knowledge, self-control, endurance, godliness, mutual affection, and love—all of these virtues require my conscious effort. I choose friends who also have these attributes, and I gain a clearer understanding of the healthy, happy person God calls me to be.

God does not want me to be abused emotionally or physically. I refuse to cultivate the insanity that comes from living with abusive people. No longer do I enter into crazy relationships and then wait for the destruction to end. I place my life in God's hands.

I seek people who support my growth as I make every effort to support them. Together we nurture one another to grow in the manifestation of faith and love.

Today I enter into honest relationships based on mutual respect and love.

---🍂---

OCTOBER 7   *CHANGE*

This is the day that the Lord has made; let us rejoice and be glad in it.   —Psalm 118:24

Autumn brings change. This autumn day I rejoice in the changes all around me—changes in the weather, the color of leaves, and the habits of creatures great and small.

I am also aware of the changes taking place within me. Day by day, little by little, I sense the nip and tug of change. Some changes involve large areas of my life. Other changes bring only minor adaptations to my life. I now step back to assess the changes taking place in this time of harvest. I enjoy the fruits of my labor and take satisfaction in the bounty of good that surrounds me.

Just as leaves turn brilliant colors, I, too, sense the artistry of God's power in my life. I rejoice that I am capable of making the needed changes and of adapting to new ways of being and doing. I feel at home in the midst of change.

I rejoice and take pleasure in the ME God continues to create.

OCTOBER 8   WISDOM

Your word is a lamp to my feet and a light to my path.
—Psalm 119:105

My feet are on a steady course and my path is well lit. I am living in ways that bring peace, stability, and happiness. I know that, unlike other creatures in the world, I have the ability to modify my life patterns. I may not be able to change the past, but I can make decisions for today that will alter what transpires in the present and future. I do not remain locked into places, relationships, or attitudes that jeopardize my sense of well-being.

Looking back over my life I see the mistakes and bad choices I have made. Now I listen, reflect, and learn from my mistakes. I see what needs to be changed, and I take the necessary steps. I will not tolerate conditions that cause me to stumble around in the dark and stub my toe.

God offers me guidance and light. Life's burdens are lifted as I go forth today doing God's will. My path is well lit for the journey ahead.

Today, and each day, I walk in the light of Christ, and my way is made clear.

OCTOBER 9   *JOY*

*Blessed be the name of the Lord from this time on
and forevermore. From the rising of the sun to its setting the name of the Lord is to be praised.*

—*Psalm 113:2-3*

I step off the treadmill of time and capture
the joy of this new day. Just as the sun rises
from its resting place, so also I rise to joyfully
meet new possibilities and promise.

There was a time in my life when I forgot
what joy felt like. I had lived in pain for so
long that I thought pain was all there was to
life. Of course, I now know that pain is a necessary part of life if I am to experience growth.
But I also know that pain is not all there is.

Joy is an essential part of each day. Today I
reach out and capture the joy that is ever present. Just as I need rest and nutrition, so also I
need joy and laughter in my day. I face today's
experiences with a joyful attitude, lighter
heart, and better perspective.

I welcome joy into my life.

Then they cried to the Lord in their trouble, and he saved them from their distress; he brought them out of darkness and gloom, and broke their bonds asunder.
—*Psalm 107:13-14*

A storm may brew today, bringing with it fierce wind and relentless rain. Sometimes a storm arises out of nowhere; other times a storm simmers and builds steam before finally hitting home. Whatever storm comes today, I remain calm. My job may take a new turn, people may do the unexpected, and situations may turn out to be different from what I had expected; but I remain at peace.

After the storm passes, I take time to assess what has transpired. The storm may have cleared the way for me to move on to new responsibilities and challenges. Or the storm may have created barriers to be overcome. Whatever has happened, I rejoice and congratulate myself for weathering the storm and for knowing that the next one will be a little bit easier.

I weather the storm today knowing that, with God's help, I can deal with whatever blows my way.

OCTOBER 11   *LOVE*

For this is the message you have heard from the beginning, that we should love one another.

—*1 John 3:11*

I am profoundly changed because I am loved. By accepting this love, I am able to be more open to others' needs and to live with deeper compassion. Love positively affects my response to life. When I offer a loving response to a friend, colleague, or even a stranger, I powerfully influence the interactions between us.

When I treat someone I dislike with disdain, I only invite the same. When I criticize others, I find I am equally hard on myself. But when I take a loving posture which elicits a loving response, the other person becomes warmer.

Bringing love into a situation makes it more bearable. Love puts me in touch with God's presence in my life and gives me the assuring strength, understanding, and patience I need.

I am changed by love.

OCTOBER 12 WISDOM

"See, I am sending you out like sheep into the midst of wolves; so be wise as serpents and innocent as doves."
—*Matthew 10:16*

As I grow in years, I grow in wisdom. Wisdom comes as I age and mature in Christ. Wisdom is knowing that all is well in the midst of a storm and that "this too shall pass." I trust more and more that God will see me through. So I relax, secure in the presence of God.

When my heart is broken by a loved one, I think I can't go on. When I am rejected by a friend, the pain is unbearable. When I lose a loved one, I am in deep despair. But the joy of wisdom is that I am able to accept difficult situations more quickly, allowing them to contribute to my wholeness even though I am in the midst of turmoil.

I've come a long way! Life has taught me what I need to know. In wisdom I take the ups and downs more easily, knowing that the pain of the present will open the way to serenity.

With the joy of wisdom, I can look at my life in a true light.

—— ❧ ——

OCTOBER 13   PEACE

Therefore, beloved, while you are waiting for these things, strive to be found by him at peace.
—*2 Peter 3:14*a

I have faith to meet the new day and whatever confronts me. Peace is mine, now and always, when I proceed with the strength of Christ to bolster me. New friends, new jobs, or new situations may elicit old fears, but fear's powerful hold on me is gone. I face nothing alone. What relief this simple truth brings! Peace through faith in Jesus is mine.

At one time my search for peace was desperate and unending. My fears overwhelmed me, and peace eluded me. Now I have the peace of Jesus Christ in my life, yet there are moments, even now, when that peace eludes me. I need to be reminded that peace will return when I take courage and act in faith. Peace, well-being, and serene joy will accompany my every step when I act in God's strength.

I accept the gift of peace when I have courage to meet the day head on, handling whatever confronts me.

OCTOBER 14   *TRUST*

*Even though I walk through the darkest valley, I fear
no evil; for you are with me; your rod and your
staff—they comfort me.*   —Psalm 23:4

Today I touch the future in trust. When I
take time to listen to a child, teach someone a
new concept, or awaken my own senses to a
new understanding, I do much more than
merely transfer information: I share my trust
in God's tomorrow.

I want to grow, and I am beckoned toward
new horizons. To grow means that I may need
to understand a new concept or theory, meet
new friends, or even relocate. I listen to the
inner guidance of the Holy Spirit urging me to
follow. God's Spirit will not lead me astray.

For many years I quelled the Spirit's urging
because I feared the new or different. Fortu-
nately, God never gave up on me. The fears
still come from time to time, but I am able to
move through them because I trust the Holy
Spirit. Now I know there is meaning in my
existence.

**I trust the urging of the Holy Spirit, who
guides my steps.**

OCTOBER 15   THANKFULNESS

Come, bless the Lord, all you servants of the Lord. . . .
Lift up your hands to the holy place, and bless the
Lord.   —Psalm 134:1a, 2

Today I want to live—truly live. I have only the twenty-four hours ahead of me, and in this time I renew my contract with life. Today is my day for celebration. I take the time to lift a prayer of thanksgiving, to buy myself or someone else flowers, or to do some act of kindness. Yesterday is past; tomorrow is not yet here. But today is all around me, and I don't want to miss it.

My eyes are truly open. My senses are alert to appreciate the weather, rain or shine. I take time to show my family my appreciation and love. Even my cat or dog receives special attention today.

I choose to do one task today that I've been putting off. Perhaps it will be something small, but it will give me a sense of accomplishment. I will not allow another day to slip by. "Carpe diem!" life screams at me. "Seize the day!" That's good advice!

I lift up my hands and bless the Lord for this day before me.

OCTOBER 16   SELF-ACCEPTANCE

Beloved, we are God's children now; what we will be has not yet been revealed. What we do know is this: when he is revealed, we will be like him, for we will see him as he is.   —1 John 3:2

Life is in process, and so am I. I like the person I see in the mirror, but I realize that part of appreciating myself is knowing that I am not the person I will be in the future. God is continually at work, helping me to become the best I can be.

Sometimes I look back on days past and wish I could change what I did or said. But the past is gone, and I cannot change it. What I can do today is reap the benefits of my experiences. So I forgive myself for my lack of judgment or oversight and ask for God's forgiveness. Sometimes I need to reconcile with a person or incident; other times things cannot be reconciled, and I must move on and, perhaps, live with the consequences. Today I step into life with confidence and choose to live in the present.

Today I move on to become the person God intends me to be.

I wait for the Lord, . . . my soul waits for the Lord more than those who watch for the morning.
—*Psalm 130:5a, 6a*

Today I live in the waiting moment of God's peace. Peacefully I not only accept but also celebrate the twists and turns of my life. I wait and trust God's guidance and blessing each day.

My acknowledgment of the many things I do not control is the first step to claiming God's peace. I may not be able to control everything, but I can help to control my attitude.

There is peace in my attitude today. Sometimes I can take action; other times I must wait and watch. No doubt peace may elude me time and again, but I now let my mind rest. I allow serenity's moment to wash over me.

Today I wait for the Lord.

---- 🍂 ----

OCTOBER 18   DISCIPLESHIP

Do not love the world or the things in the world. The love of the Father is not in those who love the world.
—1 John 2:15

If I am to be remembered, I hope I am remembered for the compassion I demonstrate, the honesty I express, and the love I extend to others. These are the important things in life.

There are occasions of the past that I'm not proud of. Even now I still do things I later regret. Yet today I begin with a fresh slate and take on new opportunities. My goal is progress, not perfection.

Today I begin anew. With a clear mind and clean conscience, I seek fresh opportunities to spread good news and witness to God's presence in the world. I find activities that take me beyond myself. As I look forward to the hours ahead, I anticipate living in respectful, Christ-like ways.

I love and work in the world to make it truly God's.

OCTOBER 19   GOD'S WILL

The Lord will keep your going out and your coming in from this time on and forevermore. —Psalm 121:8

I want what God wants for me. What God desires for me in this moment is growth and peace. When I recognize this fact and align my life with God's will, I am at peace.

In the past I tried to control situations until I managed to force the outcome I desired. Only later did I realize this outcome failed to offer the happiness I'd hoped for. I wish now I had heeded the clues, recognizing that what I sought was not God's will after all. I now know that when I force into manifestation what I want, ignoring what God wants, I usually end up with something other than what I've longed for.

I know God's will when I am still and listen. When I allow prayer and reflection to direct my efforts and I do what God wants, I find the peace I've longed for.

Today I strive to be in tune with God's will.

Whoever says, "I am in the light," while hating a brother or sister, is still in the darkness. Whoever loves a brother or sister lives in the light.

—1 John 2:9-10a

At any moment I can form the attitude to love or to hate. Just as I can choose to love and find good in others, so also I can choose to hate and reject people.

When I look for good in other people, I generally find it. When I look for bad in others, I usually find that, too. My attitudes greatly influence what I see.

Today I look for and recognize the divine spark in others. Through them I experience God's presence. What a thrill it is for me to leave my judgmentalism behind and bond with other loving people. Because of others I am part of a divine experience today.

Today I look for and find God's love and light in the people I meet.

And let us consider how to provoke one another to love and good deeds, not neglecting to meet together, as is the habit of some. —Hebrews 10:24-25a

I can't survive without relationships: some casual, some close, and some intimate. It's important to have shared moments and experiences and simply to be present for another person. This communion with other people is a celebration of life and God which lifts my spirits and lets me know that I am not alone.

Companionship is essential if I am to continue to make progress in my journey of discipleship. Being there for someone and knowing someone understands my fears give me strength to go on.

Each day I look for opportunities to give of myself as well as to receive what others have to share. I set aside time to be with my family, friends, and faith community. I have a primary responsibility to myself and the people I care about: to spend time in their presence and to share myself with them.

I find growth and affirmation in the company I keep.

OCTOBER 22   DISAPPOINTMENTS

We also boast in our sufferings, knowing that suffering produces endurance, and endurance produces character, and character produces hope, and hope does not disappoint us.   —Romans 5:3-5a

Day by day I make past and present disappointments into new possibilities. People let me down, my job does not measure up, and even promising vacations and holidays leave me wanting.

Today, with God's help, I remove roadblocks that keep me from being content in my relationships and vocation. I refuse to allow misadventures to place a cloud over future plans.

I learn from my disappointments. Disappointments help me understand how I need to change and how my relationships need to be strengthened. There are many things I do well; other things are difficult for me, and I seek the help I need. There is much I cannot control, yet in all things I do the best I can and then roll with the punches.

Today I set cynicism aside and think on new possibilities.

OCTOBER 23   BEHAVIOR

Beloved, do not imitate what is evil but imitate what is good.
                              —3 John 1:11a

My behavior tells other people, and me, a lot about myself. When I act in selfish ways, thinking only of my own good, I am not behaving in ways that will bring good into my life. What goes around comes around. My behavior elicits the responses I receive.

Today I behave in ways that attract good. I look for healthy role models and study how these individuals live their lives. I watch how Christian women and men I admire handle difficult situations, use their authority, and interact with people. From these persons I learn valuable lessons and adapt my own behavior to more healthy ways of living.

I'm thankful that God has placed mentors in my life from whom I can learn.

OCTOBER 24 CONFIDENCE

O God, my heart is steadfast; I will sing and make melody. Awake, my soul! Awake, O harp and lyre! I will awaken the dawn. —*Psalm 108:1b-2*

Today I am fully awake, confident that with every prayer I make and every step I take I am becoming stronger and more alert to the world around me. God has a plan for my life, and I stretch with new flexibility to meet it.

When I give daily attention to the nourishment I need, I live in hope-filled expectation. Confidence, strength, and freedom from fear continue to root and grow in my life. I remain on a steady course toward fulfillment as one of God's people. My confidence may waver on occasion, but I know I can ask God for the strength to act in confident ways.

Today I have the confidence to dare to be myself.

OCTOBER 25   *PEACE*

Be content with what you have; for he has said, "I will never leave you or forsake you."   —Hebrews 13:5b

My relationship with God gives me peace. Through prayer, the door of contentment is opened. In the stillness of prayer I find contentment with myself and the world.

Restlessness, on the other hand, is born of frustration. When I mistakenly think that a new home, a different job, or a new relationship will fill all my needs, I am mistaken. When I make quick changes to subdue my restlessness, these feelings simply accompany me to my new surroundings.

Sometimes restlessness is an indication of my distance from God. When I experience life in the company of God, I am able to stop the cycle of restlessness and allow peace to return to my life. I rest in a God who never leaves me. God is a constant presence in my day on whom I depend.

I am content with my life and at peace with myself and God.

OCTOBER 26   *LOVE*

If we love one another, God lives in us, and his love is
perfected in us.   —1 John 4:12b

The most important thing God asks of me is
to love other people. I am connected to others,
and all of us are connected to one another;
therefore, I must try to act in loving ways as I
interact with others. When I find it hard to
love, perhaps I simply need to avoid hurting
anyone. I have a dream that if each of us
avoided hurting one another just for one day,
the world could be transformed.

So today I act in loving ways toward myself
and the many people around me. Unlike other
days when I wait for family, co-workers, and
friends to love me first before I extend any
sign of love, today I reach out in unconditional love. As I focus on other people's needs
and give of myself, I am transformed. Love is
the transforming factor, and I give myself to it
completely.

I meet the day head on with love.

OCTOBER 27 *FAITH*

*Now faith is the assurance of things hoped for, the
conviction of things not seen.* —*Hebrews 11:1*

Being faith-filled takes effort. I must take
time in my life to foster faith. Setting aside
quiet times each day to talk with God and listen is essential. The opposite of living in the
assurance of faith is living in fear. I cannot
live in fear day after day and then wake up one
day and say, "I now have faith!" It doesn't
work that way. Each day I take little steps of
faith so that when the bigger trials come, I
will have nurtured the faith necessary to meet
them.

Life's difficulties are made easier when I
live in faith. I can handle a frightening situation, an interview, an exam, or a disagreement
with a friend when I let my faith work within
me. But first, with God's help I must work to
gain and keep the faith I need.

**I have faith in God, and I know that this part-
nership will carry me through the difficult
times.**

Beloved, since God loved us so much, we also ought to love one another.   —*1 John 4:11*

Today I am inspired to act in loving ways. As I encounter new situations with old and new friends, I gain new opportunities to perform acts of kindness.

"We may never pass this way again" goes the song. This knowledge heightens the importance of each encounter. Knowing there is much to be gained from each person, I find inspiration every step along the way.

To be inspired to love means that I must be fully present with each person. It feels good to express love as I smile, touch, or pray. I feel more vital and more alive. Love heals, strengthens, and gives me and others the courage to go on.

Today I am lovingly inspired to make each encounter matter.

OCTOBER 29   *LOVE*

God is love, and those who abide in love abide in God, and God abides in them.   —*1 John 4:16*

The more I am in concert with God's love, the more my own love is strengthened. I nurture God's presence within me through daily prayer and reflection. This allows the flame of love to flicker and grow bright.

There were times in my life when the flame of love almost went out. I felt alone and abandoned, as if God had left me. In times of grief and rejection, I thought I never would be able to love again.

Now, in partnership with God, I am learning to love once again. The more I rely on God to see me through these difficult times, the more certain I am that I have the love to make it through any experience.

When my flame of love is burning low, I turn to God who helps me rekindle the flame.

OCTOBER 30   FAITH

And this is the victory that conquers the world, our faith.
                                      —*1 John* 5:4b

Victory belongs to those who dare to live boldly in faith. When I answer the call and accept the opportunity, I am able to take the first step to reach my goal.

Many times I haved promised myself that I would do something, but then I fail to follow through with my plans. Because of my own lack of faith, I have seen too much pessimism, too much negativism, and too many defeats.

Faith in God's purpose for my life undergirds all that I undertake. My positive attitude, which is grounded in faith, carries over into new possibilities for life. God wants me to live victoriously, but I must have faith *and* take action. Today I am ready to put forth the necessary effort.

In faith I move toward the fulfillment of my dreams.

—— ❧ ——

OCTOBER 31   AUTHENTICITY

*Let us love, not in word or speech, but in truth and
action.*   —1 John 3:18

I live authentically when my actions as
well as my words are grounded in truth.
Today I accept responsibility for the person I
am becoming and for the way I live each day.
The temptation to blame others for my
choices or dilemmas is always present, but I
do not waste time placing blame for my decisions and actions.

There are innumerable truthful reasons I
could give to explain why I am the way I am,
but none of these is empowering. It's unhelpful for me to replay these excuses over and
over like a broken record.

Today I have numerous options to choose
from as I chart my course. I make choices that
heighten my sense of well-being and positively influence my day. Today I act on these
choices in truth and love.

**I am an authentic follower of Christ when my
speech and actions are grounded in truth and
love.**

NOVEMBER 1   LOVE

And this is his commandment, that we should believe in the name of his Son Jesus Christ and love one another, just as he has commanded us. —1 John 3:23

Love is what quiets my spirit and calls me to be gentle with others. I support my friends in love when they celebrate their successes or fail in their endeavors.

No one wants to be taken for granted. We all need recognition to assure us that we are not being overlooked. Today I assure my loved ones that they are needed, appreciated, and loved. Likewise, others assure me of my specialness when they reach out to me in loving ways. Who I am and what I do are valued by others. I gain strength from those who support my endeavors.

I quiet my spirit today so that I can both give and receive love.

Now to him who is able to keep you from falling . . . to the only God our Savior, through Jesus Christ our Lord, be glory, majesty, power, and authority;...now and forever. Amen.   —Jude 1:24a, 25

Each of us has miraculously been summoned to the road of discipleship. At times I feel like a hopeless disciple, aimless and out of step; but, miraculously, though I stumble I do not fall. The help and guidance I need always comes, usually in the form of another person. Today I appreciate God's gracious miracle in my life.

I still have days when the going is rough; days when I feel immature and unable to handle responsibility; days when I need a mother to take me under her wing and assure me that everything will be all right. When these days come, I look to God and others for help. I also pause to reflect on how far I've come. Today I see miracles at work in my life as well as in the lives of other people on the road of discipleship, and I have hope.

I live in hope today as I reflect on the miracle that I've come this far.

NOVEMBER 3 FRIENDSHIP

Let mutual love continue. —Hebrews 13:1

The gift of friendship is a gift I give myself. In years past, friends often were missing from my life. Of course, I had friends here and there, but I questioned whether I could really trust them. I wondered how I could trust someone else when I didn't even trust myself.

Friendship entails the risk of being vulnerable; it means making the decision to trust and to be trustworthy. Even so, friendship is worth all the risk and uncertainty, for without friends my life would be empty. Shared experiences bring joys that otherwise would be missing from my life. The friends in my life give me intimate companionship for the journey.

Today I thank God for my friends, and I pick up the phone or pen to say hello to them.

❦

NOVEMBER 4   SELF-EXAMINATION

I was glad when they said to me, "Let us go to the house of the Lord!"   —*Psalm 122:1*

Today I slow down and take time to appreciate my relationship with God and myself. I've always been in such a hurry, as if I were engaged in a race against time. I was in a hurry to get through school, to get married (or unmarried), and to get where I am today. I've been so rushed that I've not even had time for myself. I've been the dutiful child, or compassionate friend, or selfless parent, but how often have I been myself?

Today I slow my pace to examine who I am and what I really want. I don't want to get trapped in playing a part. So I take time to be myself. It feels good to step back from the craziness of the world and live life at a sane pace. It's so easy to get caught up in spirit-crushing business. I don't have to, and I won't! Today I pause and say, "Let's go into the house of the Lord."

Today I slow down and take life at a steady pace.

Then the woman left her water jar and went back to the city. She said to the people, "Come and see a man who told me everything I have ever done."

—John 4:28-29

Today I turn over a new leaf and begin again.

Sometimes I feel that it would be better just to pack my bags and start over someplace else. Sometimes I feel as if I'll never convince others I've changed. Sometimes I feel as if I've been humiliated in front of too many people, and everyone thinks of me as a failure. Sometimes I guess I think of myself as a failure, too.

Today I say, "Rubbish!" Like the woman of Samaria, I can face and admit what I've done. I can and I will stay and make things right. I must face my problem and forgive myself. Running away won't help; it will only make me feel more ashamed than ever. I know it will be hard to face my problem, but, with God's help, I will overcome it by accepting what has happened and beginning again.

I begin again today by putting the pieces of my life back together.

NOVEMBER 6 — TRIALS

I lift up my eyes to the hills—from where will my help come? My help comes from the Lord, who made heaven and earth.
—Psalm 121:1-2

In times of trouble and distress I call on God for the help I need, and time and time again God's presence is made known to me. Of course, I do not enjoy suffering or pain, but difficult times have led me to better understand how fortunate I am and how infinitely rich my life is. Difficult times put life in perspective. I'm able to sort out, with a clear mind, what is important and what is not.

When I worry, I miss the gifts of life that can be mine. When I am preoccupied with what *might* happen, I miss out on what *is* happening. Today I live in this moment and capture all the richness it holds. I never know where the special gift of today will lie. Therefore, I remain open to the tapestry of possibilities opening before me.

In the midst of trouble, I lift up my eyes to receive God's gifts.

NOVEMBER 7   FRIENDSHIP

May mercy, peace, and love be yours in abundance.
—*Jude 1:2*

God wants mercy, peace, and love to be mine in abundance. So today I abundantly surround myself with people who are supportive and caring. I plan activities with people whom I enjoy and who appreciate me. I choose friendships in which there is mutual caring and sharing.

I include time for good friends and fellowship in my social calendar today. I do not place on my calendar occasions that have the potential of producing anxiety or tension. If I must attend a family or work-related event that causes me stress, I take along a trusted friend and go on my terms.

In whatever way I choose to spend my social time, I make sure it is healthy for me. I resolve to have a social life that is happy and full. As I turn my attention to God, I am shown a new way to live and experience life.

I spend my leisure time in happy, confidence-building ways.

—— 🍂 ——

NOVEMBER 8   RELATIONSHIPS

O give thanks to the Lord, for he is good; his steadfast love endures forever!
                                    —Psalm 118:1

God is good, steadfast in love and enduring forever. God is perfect, because God is God. But others in my life are human, and humans are imperfect. They are not always good, nor is their love unwavering.

Today I examine my expectations and realize that people make mistakes and have shortcomings just as I do. I let go of my belief that trusting others always brings pain. I also let go of the false belief that if people say they love me, they will never bring me pain.

Just because I was hurt in the past does not mean that I cannot love again. I'm realistic enough to know that sometimes people hurt one another. I may need to forgive the hurt caused by a person and move on to a new place in our relationship.

Today I live in realistic grace with others.

May the Lord, maker of heaven and earth, bless you from Zion.
         —Psalm 134:3

Today I remember that I am blessed even in the midst of trials. When I encounter problems, I pray and rest assured that solutions are close at hand. Praying with confidence and expectation helps me to relax and to consider the circumstance with a clear mind and calm emotions. Then I am able to look at all the dimensions of the problem and the various ways it might be solved.

Some solutions require quick, easy action. Other solutions take time and involve many intricate steps. I have the creative capability to look at the circumstances from different perspectives and to choose the best course of action.

Problems are a normal part of life; solving problems also is a normal part of life. I welcome the opportunity to use my creative, flexible self to engage and solve the problems that arise today.

I find blessings even as I take on and solve the problems I encounter.

Then he said to the man, "Stretch out your hand."
He stretched it out, and it was restored, as sound as
the other.   —Matthew 12:13

Jesus wants me to be a restored, whole person. My health is one area of my life in which I must participate in this restoration process. If I've put off my yearly check-up with my physician, I make the appointment now. My dental needs are no exception. I need to take the time to care for my teeth.

Adequate exercise and sound nutrition go hand in hand. Today I choose to exercise—perhaps go for a brisk walk. I sit down to eat unhurriedly, rather than grab a quick snack from the machine.

I am conscious of my good health and grateful for the freedom it gives me. I reach out my hand and am thankful for the ability to grasp. I stand on my feet and acknowledge the ability to walk unencumbered.

I care for the body God has given me so that I can enjoy the days to come.

NOVEMBER 11   REVERENCE

His divine power has given us everything needed for
life and godliness.   —2 Peter 1:3a

What a blessing to be part of God's creation!
God's divine power has given me everything I
need to live a rich, full life. I am ever mindful
of the strength and nurture that are always at
hand. I am gratefully reminded that God is
with me and all is well. When I feel distanced
from God, I ask myself, "Who moved?" Today
I pray for the wisdom to stay close to my Creator.

When I was a child, I envisioned God as a
"candy man"—an old man in the sky who
gave me what I wanted. As a teenager, I
rebelled against God, questioning God's power
and will. Then there came a time when I was
too busy for God.

Now I'm thankful that even in my rebellion
and neglect, God never was very far away. I
realize that God is in control and watches
over me every day.

I am thankful that God's divine power follows
me everywhere I go.

NOVEMBER 12 COMMUNITY

How very good and pleasant it is when kindred live together in unity!
—*Psalm 133:1*

The love and sympathy of friends help me in my discipleship journey. As I also accompany others, I find companionship for my own daily walk. I'm fortunate to have a Christian community to support and cushion my fall, should it come. But more important, I have the examples of others to inspire me.

As we love and support one another, we actively call for responsibility, accountability, and discipleship. We ask one another: "Does our behavior agree with our beliefs? Are we living the values we profess?" As we reach out in love, we help one another search for solutions. With others I give my assumptions a "reality check" as I journey toward integrity.

How thankful I am to have such a group of people! We truly count in one anothers' lives.

Today I am thankful for the community of friends who accompany me on my journey.

NOVEMBER 13   *PRAYER*

Are any among you suffering? They should pray.
                                        —*James 5:13*a

No answer eludes me when I turn to the source of all answers—God. Prayer accompanied by reflection provides the answers I need for whatever I must face. The answers I want are not guaranteed, but I trust that I will be directed to take the right steps. It is well with my soul as I commit my will to God's care and direction.

It's comforting to know that God is always close at hand. But at times I fail to quiet myself long enough to heed God's message. My mind races, and the answer I seek recedes further into the background with each new focus that captures my attention.

The process is simple if I'm willing to follow. The answer is there when I'm ready to listen. Being a disciple of Jesus means sitting quietly and asking God for the guidance I hunger for.

I find time today to sit in quiet, to be still, and to listen.

"God is spirit, and those who worship him must worship in spirit and truth."   —*John 4:24*

Spirit and truth connect us all. In Christ we are one body. As I come to understand the role of my connectedness to others as part of God's plan for all creation, my fear of other people subsides.

I, in truth, have learned who I am by closely observing my behavior toward other people in my life. Others are a true reflection of who I am. Sometimes they reflect parts of myself that I have not yet learned to love or trust. In connection I am urged and encouraged to trust and have faith in others, resting in the knowledge that our Creator is in control.

Fear creates a false sense of isolation. Today I smile upon the wholeness of life without fear. Because we are connected by Jesus Christ, we all are one, connected with God in spirit and in truth.

I rejoice that, through God, I am connected to others in spirit and truth.

NOVEMBER 15   PARENTING

I have no greater joy than this, to hear that my children are walking in the truth.   —3 John 1:4

I, like God, want my children to be happy, healthy individuals. I feel great joy when I hear that my children are doing well and walking in the truth.

I live my life knowing that my children are separate individuals with their own thoughts, emotions, and behaviors. I do not control them, nor do they control me. My children have their shortcomings and faults, just as I have mine. My children also have qualities worthy of praise and do the best they can, just as I do. I can model the behaviors and attitudes I want my children to have, but I cannot control their thoughts and emotions. My children are wonderfully and uniquely made.

My task today is to affirm my children's independence and to see their positive attributes. I affirm my ability to guide them in healthy, loving, encouraging ways.

I respect and love the children God has entrusted to me.

By the rivers of Babylon—there we sat down and there we wept when we remembered Zion.

—Psalm 137:1a

God has given me the strength and capabilities to work toward the completeness I seek. I know that there are no "quick fixes" or magic solutions to difficult problems, but with God at my side, I have the resources I need to meet whatever life brings.

There are times when I feel an inner emptiness, leading me to feelings of despair and disappointment. I suffer, thinking I'm the only one who feels this way. When I look to one person, job, or event to fix what's wrong, I end up feeling worse than when I began.

I remind myself that I do not have to suffer. I am confident that I can find solutions to my problems. I am ready to work on the root causes of my distress, even if this is the longer route to finding solutions. And I am ready to make my readiness known to God and others who will be able to provide the help I need.

I am whole and complete even as I suffer and seek answers to life's difficult questions.

And the Word became flesh and lived among us, and we have seen his glory, the glory as of a father's only son, full of grace and truth. —John 1:14

I have lived long enough in the cave of despair and depression. I am ready to meet joy. I now know that my life is a reflection of God's glory, grace, and truth. Looking out with new eyes, I see blue skies, vibrant sunlight, and a prism of color: yellow flowers, red birds, and green grass. Fresh scents and sights promise me sunny days ahead.

My time spent in dreariness was not in vain. Looking at my past has given me fresh insight into why I am who I am. Now I move on. With a spring in my step and bounce in my gait, I walk out of the dreariness and pain. I'm learning once again how to laugh, play, and love. Soon I will be able to embrace my joy just as easily as I took hold of the pain. Soon, very soon, I will accept the loveliness of my joy.

I welcome joy into my life.

NOVEMBER 18 RESPONSIBILITY

In the beginning was the Word, and the Word was with God, and the Word was God. —John 1:1

I'm glad there are some things in life that are constant. God is constant, and God gives me the unwavering foundation I need. I can relax as I live the beauty of this new day. I remind myself that I am not responsible for all the people or situations around me. I do not always have to make the coffee, remember everyone's birthday, or break the silence at meetings.

I'm not "on duty" twenty-four hours a day, making sure that everyone is comfortable and that every detail is cared for. It's too exhausting to live this way, and I refuse to do it anymore.

Starting today, I allow others to take responsibility. I do what I can in a sensible way and at a reasonable rate of speed. My time to enjoy life is NOW!

With God as my constant foundation, I relax and enjoy the beauty of each day.

🍎

"If any want to become my followers, let them deny themselves and take up their cross daily and follow me."
—Luke 9:23

As a follower of Jesus, I take up crosses daily; but I do not take them up alone. There are other disciples, whom I call my friends, who walk with me on this journey. My sense of purpose in community opens wide the door that allows my energy and enthusiasm to flow.

As the adventure of this day unfolds, I have the energy to meet it. Being a member of this community brings order to my life and allows me to fully experience love, joy, harmony, and peace. My life takes on new meaning as I learn to see others' needs and cares. Side by side with other followers I can meet the challenge.

As the sun sets on this day, I am content in knowing that I have lived this day in the company of others who also live with purpose in their lives. My daily cross has been lightened by those who share my life.

I rest in peacefulness tonight knowing that in the morning I will rise, with others, to once again serve Christ.

He said to them, "But who do you say that I am?"
Peter answered, "The Messiah of God."   —*Luke 9:20*

Jesus asked his disciples who people were saying he was. I, like Jesus, also wonder who people think I am. In the past I was afraid of what they might say, so I never showed them the real me. Now I introduce the real me to those I meet, rather than a reflection of who I think they want me to be. In this way I embrace my own needs and feelings.

I accept that I am imperfect and that I need others. Acknowledging my humanness and my needs frees me from playing a part that doesn't fit. Today I take time to examine who I am and how I let others know the true me. I proudly live the real me. The real me now stands up!

I accept myself, knowing that others also accept me.

NOVEMBER 21   *CHANGE*

*Grow in the grace and knowledge of our Lord and
Savior Jesus Christ.*   *—2 Peter 3:18a*

Today I ask God for guidance as I move forward with confidence in each activity. Problems do not daunt me but spur me on to creative solutions. I am challenged to expand my capabilities, and with each challenge I grow in grace and knowledge.

What growth do I anticipate today? Do I welcome the experiences that bring growth--intellectually, emotionally, and spiritually? Or have I grown lethargic and apathetic toward life, settling for the status quo? Growth means change. Do I want to make changes? Change is seldom easy, but I must change if I am to mature as a disciple of Jesus.

I can't grow and change by myself, but I have God and supportive friends to help me. The going won't be easy, but support and guidance are available if I seek them. Today I make the decision for growth through change.

I make choices that lead me to grow in grace and knowledge.

NOVEMBER 22   COMPASSION

The Lord is gracious and merciful, slow to anger
and abounding in steadfast love.   —Psalm 145:8

Today I reconnect with my compassionate self. Compassion—being filled with grace, mercy, and love—is not gone from my life; it is only in need of resurrection. My home or work situation may be hard or ruthless, but I make the choice to live by a different standard—the standard of discipleship—rather than to fall prey to what appears inevitable.

Living as a disciple of Jesus means waking up each morning and liking what I see in the mirror. I see a person who is compassionate and loving toward others. I am in touch with the spirit of God in myself and others, and I express my care and mercy time and time again. My heart is overflowing with care and compassion.

Today I open my heart once again and live in compassion for God's world.

We give you thanks, O Lord, with my whole heart; before the gods I sing your praise; On the day I called, you answered me, you increased my strength of soul. —Psalm 138:1, 3

My soul is strengthened as I get in touch with God. This strength of soul is not a power over others but the power of the Holy Spirit glowing from within. Accepting this power and strength is essential as I come to know and understand myself. When I claim this power, I move toward becoming all that God wants me to be.

My strength and power come as I discover who I am and dare to act on this knowledge. As I accept me for me, I tap into the power that God has given me and find strength for whatever comes today.

Today I claim God's power.

NOVEMBER 24 COMMUNICATING

Above all, my beloved, do not swear . . . but let your "Yes" be yes and your "No" be no. —*James 5:12*

Starting today I take a small step in adopting a new strategy for my participation in God's world by communicating more effectively.

When I speak, I am careful to see that others are sure of where I stand. When I listen, I am careful to understand others' points of view. As I examine my conversations today, I look to see if I: (1) give others my full attention, (2) listen without interrupting, (3) focus on the subject at hand, (4) give an adequate and complete response, and (5) remain physically and mentally attentive until the conversation has ended. All of these tactics improve communication and show that I really value what others have to say.

Today I choose to respond in loving, sensitive ways to my spouse, children, and colleagues. If I am to know what others need, then I must take time in conversations to listen and communicate—to set clear boundaries and let my "Yes" be yes and my "No" be no.

Today I begin to communicate anew.

NOVEMBER 25   THANKFULNESS

Let us make a joyful noise to the rock of our salvation! Let us come into his presence with thanksgiving.
—Psalm 95:1b-2a

Today I give thanks. If "thank you" is the only prayer I say today, it is enough. "Thank you" completes the circle between Creator and creation and announces that I'm open to receive the gifts God gives with an open heart. In gratitude I realize that only through thanksgiving do I become a follower of Jesus.

Sitting here in a prayerful frame of mind, I remember the past with fondness and anticipate the promise of the future, but I center my attention on this present moment. The experiences of today are here only for today. Now, in the midst of my activity, I give God thanks for my life, knowing all I experience adds to my knowledge and growth. I am filled with joy and opportunity as I live in the here and now!

I am thankful for the blessings I receive today.

NOVEMBER 26   *CREATIVITY*

You will know the truth, and the truth will make you free.
—*John 8:32*

Today I open myself to the creative ways people express themselves: notes from friends, a beautifully decorated room, poetry, photography, or cooking. I take seriously the communication of individuals which gives life joy and meaning.

I also open my ears and heart to people who, like Jesus, are the "truth-tellers" of today. Sometimes people need to express things in creative new ways so that old ideas may be heard. These persons' perceptions, experiences, and interpretations deserve to be heard and taken seriously. These are courageous people who dare to give accounts from an unpopular point of view.

I also am called upon to be a "truth-teller," and I express this truth in many creative ways: planting an herb garden, sewing new drapes, or working with wood. In these ways I express what I think the world should be like and how I should live in God's created order.

I, like Jesus, become a "truth-teller" as I communicate in beautiful, creative, freeing ways.

---❦---

NOVEMBER 27   THANKFULNESS

*What shall I return to the Lord for all his bounty to
me? I will lift up the cup of salvation and call on the
name of the Lord.*   —*Psalm 116:12-13*

In this moment of clarity I am full of gratitude to God as I open my eyes and begin to see
the possibilities around me. I see the good that
I can accomplish each day as well as the good
that is directed toward me. I am thankful for
the person I am in this moment, and I am
thankful for the loved ones in my life: my
family, my friends, and the people in my community.

At one time I felt I had nothing to be thankful for. All I could see was the negative. But
today I put an end to my negativity and look
at life afresh. I truly give thanks for the good
that is in my life. In the midst of these feelings of thankfulness, I am able to see, even if
only a glimpse, what it would mean to live in
harmony with myself and those around me. In
our thankfulness for one another we would be
healed.

**Today I am open to see all my blessings, and I
am thankful.**

NOVEMBER 28 COURAGE

For there our captors asked us for songs, and our tormentors asked for mirth, saying, "Sing us one of the songs of Zion!" How could we sing the Lord's song in a foreign land?
—Psalm 137:3-4

How can I sing God's song in this foreign, strange world I live in? The song I have to sing is trivialized by those around me who do not want to hear me. They may even criticize me, saying that what I offer is not relevant but only trivial and self-serving.

I know what it feels like to be interrupted or refused the opportunity to speak. Today I set a different example when interacting with others. I suspend judgment so that all can express themselves. I take time to draw silent listeners into the discussion. I collaborate with others to come to consensus decisions instead of charging ahead with my own agenda.

Sometimes I am called to speak as an alien in a foreign land. The consequences may be high, but the consequences of not "singing God's song" may be greater. So I find the courage I need and, with Christ and my community of sisters and brothers undergirding me, I sing!

Today I have the courage to sing God's song!

—— ❦ ——

NOVEMBER 29   COMMUNICATING

Out of the depths I cry to you, O Lord. Lord, hear my voice! Let your ears be attentive to the voice of my supplications! —Psalm 130:1-2

Today I break my silence. No longer do I allow others to prevent my speech or shape and control it. I let my authentic voice emerge, expressing what I feel rather than what I think will be acceptable. I call those who have not listened to me or heard me, as well as myself, into accountability. I need to be able to adjust my hearing in order to understand people who talk differently than I do.

Today I break free from destructive, disempowering silences: denial, secrets, taboo subjects, veilings, and omissions. In Jesus Christ I am empowered to write and speak. I decide what and when I will speak and the form of communication I will use. I have the power to share my unique voice. I honor my own voice and the voices of those around me.

As an empowered person of God, I communicate with truth and authority.

NOVEMBER 30   FORGIVENESS

Search me, O God, and know my heart; test me and know my thoughts. See if there is any wicked way in me, and lead me in the way everlasting.

—*Psalm 139:23-24*

I know I am in need of forgiveness, so I search my heart and thoughts and confess my mistakes. I seek forgiveness from God and the people I've hurt. It seems I always hurt the ones I love the most. I acknowledge my responsibility for what I've done. I admit my wrongs, make amends to those I've hurt or disappointed (including myself), and move on.

I ask forgiveness and make amends—not so that others will like me or so that I can manipulate and control, but so that I can bring order to my life before God. I give my soul over to God who makes it clean.

I genuinely work to change my behavior and to move toward a Christ-centered future. I search myself, laying everything before God, so that I may feel clean and whole again. What a wonderful feeling it is to recognize past mistakes, confess my sins, accept forgiveness, and live a new day.

I begin again and stand before God as forgiven and clean.

DECEMBER 1   RELAXATION

O LORD, you have searched me and known me. You know when I sit down and when I rise up; you discern my thoughts from far away. —Psalm 139:1-2

It's comforting to know there is One who knows me through and through. I needn't bring God up-to-date each time I sit to pray, for God has searched me and known me, perhaps in ways that I have failed to know myself. Today I relax and appreciate the comfort that God's knowledge of me brings, so that I may understand myself.

In the past I took on more and more responsibility. My goal was to cram as much as possible into each day, so that I might feel productive and in control. Outside I appeared poised, confident, and calm, but inside my life was a blur.

I still live in a fast-moving world with heavy demands, and I still must move at a fairly brisk pace; but I can set healthy limits and boundaries regarding what I can and cannot do. I do not run from one task to the next but relax and savor the satisfaction that a job well-done brings.

Today I relax as I slow down and take time to know God and myself.

--- 🍂 ---

DECEMBER 2   RELAXATION

*Create in me a clean heart, O God, and put a new
and right spirit within me.*   —Psalm 51:10

Today there is a new spirit within me that
gives lightness to my day. At one time I was so
weighed down by pressures that I felt as if I was
dragging a ten-ton ball and chain. Anything that
resembled rest, relaxation, or personal down-
time was anathema. My prayer life suffered,
too. I needed action, excitement, intrigue, and
drama to feel that my life was worthwhile.

Now I realize there is nothing wrong with
giving everything to meet an important project deadline and then taking time out after-
ward. But choosing to go all out day after day
places me at a high risk of spiritual, physical,
and psychological depletion.

Because I am concerned about my fast-
paced life, I make small but significant
changes in my schedule. I spend one night
each week with myself and my family, take
up a sport or form of exercise I really love, and
cultivate a hobby such as reading or playing
music. I find quiet time every day to simply
"be" and to pray.

Today I thank God for the ability to relax.

DECEMBER 3   TRUTH

Where can I go from your spirit? Or where can I flee from your presence?
                                    —*Psalm 139:7*

There are no secrets from God. Wherever I go and whatever I do, God is there. This is a comforting thought, but it also can be a disconcerting thought! I like my secrets, but I recognize that secrets can be like invisible amoebas that slowly eat away at my soul and distort my relationships.

One of the rules in my family was never to talk, trust, or feel. Ours was a house full of secrets. Of course, all families have problems, but how we confront those problems determines the health of our souls. We are as sick as the secrets we keep.

Today I choose not to enter into bonds of secrecy with others but to live in truth. I accept responsibility for my actions and decisions so that I may become all that God wants me to be.

Today I live in truth, free from the burden of secrecy.

❦ ──────

DECEMBER 4   RELAXATION

"How often have I desired to gather your children together as a hen gathers her brood under her wings, and you were not willing!"   —Matthew 23:37b

How often I welcome God's tender wings drawing me under a loving breast to rest. I long to be cared for in God's nurturing presence. I need to feel once more the love and comfort of home. Today I am willing to surrender my worries to God who is in ultimate control.

Setting boundaries and limits for what I can responsibly do is difficult, yet I realize that limits are necessary if I am to prevent my fast-paced life from developing into a compulsion to do more and more. I hate to slow down, because I feel I have not done enough regardless of how much I accomplish. But if I slow down, then I begin to think about myself, my relationships, and how I really feel.

Today I take a first step to slow down so that I may confront my life. I take two deep breaths and relax, knowing God brings me rest in weariness. I don't have to do it all. I am good enough just being me.

I willingly lie under God's wing, knowing I am "good enough."

Those who trust in the LORD are like Mount Zion, which cannot be moved, but abides forever.
—*Psalm 125:1*

Today I trust; this is the only way I can live. It takes a lot of faith to live one day at a time, trusting God to be with me no matter what happens. But the alternative, thinking I can control everything that happens, is arrogant. Today I give up my illusions of control. I cannot control situations, others' lives, or the future.

I am fully alive as I learn to live in faith. I must do my homework, make the best decisions I can, and then let go and live. Today I take a leap of faith and walk in the uncertainty of life.

I live each day in faith and trust.

DECEMBER 6   RELAXATION

Be still before the LORD and wait patiently for him.
—Psalm 37:7a

I grew up thinking work was valuable and anything less than work was slothful. So I kept myself busy—always doing, doing, doing, until I became afraid to quit or even slow down.

I enjoy the work I do and appreciate the satisfaction it gives, but my whole life is not wrapped up in a frantic schedule. To run from task to task is workaholism, which may mean failed health or a ruined family life. The price of continuing at this pace is too high.

Today I take control of my calendar and decide what is worthy of my time. I keep the dates I've made with loved ones rather than cancel them to squeeze in yet another appointment. I look forward to the "down-time" in my week. I am unafraid to face the quiet hours of reflection and rest. I look forward to a time of rest and relaxation.

Today I follow God's example and rest from my labor.

DECEMBER 7   EXPECTATION

Ask in faith, never doubting.   —James 1:6a

I face the challenge to live expectantly in the present, believing in faith that God will hear my requests and fill my needs. Today I live and appreciate the now of this moment so that I do not miss the gateway of opportunity before me.

Opportunities must be seized in the moment, or they may slip away. My own potential for greatness may hinge on my ability to seize one important moment. Discerning that moment may be the most critical skill I need to possess.

Today I am alert to the present moment, ready to rise to meet whatever opportunity may come my way. This moment may make a major difference in my life, and I don't want to miss it!

As I live expectantly in the present, I notice and appreciate the NOW.

DECEMBER 8   GOALS

"Do not work for the food that perishes, but for the food that endures for eternal life." —John 6:27

As I work to obtain my goals, I keep in mind that goals are only temporary measures from which I operate. I can change my goals as needed to accomplish God's purpose for my life.

Sometimes I get so hung up on reaching my goals that I forget they are not solid structures. The journey or process, rather than the end product, is what really matters. I don't want to miss the fun of the journey or the joyous experiences on the road. If my life becomes all work and no play, I may miss the opportunity to rejoice in my life in Christ and be present in each moment.

So today I travel toward my goals in ways that are right for me. I do only those things that are aligned with the ultimate purpose and meaning that God has for my life.

With wholehearted enthusiasm I launch toward my goals, taking care to enjoy each step of the journey.

DECEMBER 9   PEACE

Help me, O LORD my God! Save me according to
your steadfast love.   —Psalm 109:26

Today I realize my need to be saved from
emptiness, overwhelming sadness, and the
things that can destroy my soul. Christ beck-
ons me to live within the realm of God's love.
God's love is steadfast, and I need this assurance in the uncertainty of this life.

At times I am so caught up in my work and
agenda that I do not see what a fog I'm in. My
money and successes have not given me the
serenity I need. Then I realize that "things"
outside cannot fill the emptiness inside. Being
in touch with myself and sensing my connectedness with my Creator are what give me
steadfast peace.

Today the fog lifts, and I see that what I
search for is not somewhere "out there" but
right here in my relationship with myself and
my Creator.

**Today I find peace as I step out of the fog and
take hold of the steadfast love that is mine.**

Draw near to God, and he will draw near to you.
Cleanse your hands, you sinners, and purify your
hearts, you double-minded.   —James 4:8

I've found a way to follow Jesus that is leading me to greater happiness and peace than I ever thought possible. This peace with myself, God, and others leads me to move beyond myself to share this good news.

Now I see how biblical truths and faith in God bear on my own and others' lives. God has something to say to me, and I'm ready to listen. Through listening, study, prayer, and reflection I learn what holiness is all about. As I enter the realm of the Holy, I am freed to live the meaningful life God intends. Yet holiness within my life does not stop at personal piety or inner peace. True holiness means reaching out to others and inviting them into God's realm.

The place of holiness I find in my life I now extend to others.

DECEMBER 11 FRIENDSHIP

As the mountains surround Jerusalem, so the LORD surrounds his people, from this time on and forevermore. —*Psalm 125:2*

I am not alone. I am surrounded by God. I also am surrounded by others who care. I take today as an opportunity to cultivate new relationships.

I no longer isolate myself by being judgmental of others. These are the people whom Jesus loves and for whom Jesus died. They are people worthy of my time and attention. There is much I can learn from my friends even as I share my offerings with them. I choose friends who are loving and good. Our words and actions convey a mutual respect.

God intends for me to make this journey of life with companions. So I set myself free from trying to make it alone and appreciate the caring people in my life.

I choose people to be my companions in life, for this is what God wants.

DECEMBER 12   REVERENCE

Say to God, "How awesome are your deeds!"
—Psalm 66:3a

Today I express appreciation for God's world. With awe I notice the sounds of birds in the early dawn. As the morning begins to settle, I hear the noises of children as they walk to school. Throughout my day I allow feelings of awe to fill me. How rare it is to pause in my busy day to appreciate the expansiveness of God's love, yet awe for God's love is what gives life zest.

I also have a feeling of awe for each person I meet today. Each individual is unique. His or her ideas, thoughts, and gifts bring a specialness to our task together.

I also celebrate and accept my own unique worth. I hold feelings of awe and wonderment as I, too, take my place in God's universe.

I stand in awe and wonderment.

DECEMBER 13   DISCIPLESHIP

They devoted themselves to the apostles' teaching and fellowship, to the breaking of bread and the prayers.
—*Acts 2:42*

I commit myself to the basic disciplines of discipleship. To study God's Word, pray, meet together, and share bread in the Lord's Supper with others who also are on the journey, are the basics needed to lead a life devoted to Christ.

Sometimes I find my attention and energy spinning haphazardly in other directions. I want to deny what is happening as I go farther and farther away from God. As my thinking becomes muddled, I lose my ability to make sound judgments. I fall into the same traps and make the same mistakes over and over.

It's time to get back to the basics: the Word, caring friends, good bread, and prayer. These are the basics that will give my life a healthy perspective.

I am a disciplined disciple who lives the basics of faith.

—— ❦ ——

DECEMBER 14 THANKFULNESS

Then he took a loaf of bread, and when he had given thanks, he broke it and gave it to them.

—*Luke 22:19*a

Jesus gave thanks. Surely this dinner with his disciples on the eve of his trial was a difficult moment. Yet even in that moment he gave God thanks for the good. I, too, give thanks for the blessings in my life.

Appreciation and gratitude are important to give balance to my day. There are innumerable people who have blessed my life. Some have shared their homes, and others have shared a listening ear or a smile. By sharing their wisdom, friends have made a difference in my decisions and actions.

For all the people who have come in and out of my life, I give thanks. I appreciate each one and offer my gratitude to God for their lives.

I am thankful for all God's wonderful blessings!

---- 🐦 ----

DECEMBER 15   HEALING

Lift your drooping hands and strengthen your weak knees, and make straight paths for your feet, so that what is lame may not be put out of joint, but rather be healed.   —*Hebrews 12:12-13*

With God's help I reflect upon the meaning of yesterday's hurts so that I may be healed and move on. In the past experiences overwhelmed me, and I pushed them away. Now I take them out a piece at a time, as I am able. God's Spirit shows love by releasing these memories as I am able to handle them. I have the opportunity to heal the hurts at a pace I can endure.

It takes a leap of faith to enter the unknown, yet facing the old hurts is a first step to healing. Healing takes time. I don't rush the healing but allow the wounds to be opened, cleaned, and bound up as I am able.

I am growing stronger with each day of healing.

DECEMBER 16   GIVING

"Whoever gives even a cup of cold water to one of these little ones in the name of a disciple—truly I tell you, none of these will lose their reward."

—*Matthew 10:42*

Today I give a cup of cold water. As a disciple of Jesus Christ, this means I extend myself for other people, especially children. When I see a need, I reach out to help. I am fully aware of what's going on around me, and I see the opportunity for service along the way.

At one time I looked at all the injustices and waited for God or someone else to fix whatever was wrong—and perhaps even to fix me. I believed that God could make everything all right and that all I had to do was sit back and watch it happen.

The truth is that God's work takes place through me as well as through others. When I recognize my responsibility and accept oneness with all God's creation, I take the first step toward the healing of myself and the world I live in.

Today I give a cup of cold water and become part of the healing process.

DECEMBER 17   HOPE

There was a man sent from God, whose name was John. He came as a witness to testify to the light, so that all might believe through him.   —John 1:6-7

Today I live in hope as a person of the light. I, like John, tell others about the light I've found, joyfully inviting them to explore this light for themselves. Especially when I enter into places of darkness—hopelessness, abuse, hatred, or war—I share the light that is a part of who I am as a Christian.

In the darkest corners of my life there still may lurk dark shadows, menaces, and threats. Darkness separates me from my neighbor or friend. When I step into darkness I cannot recognize the trouble within.

Today I step out of the murky shadows and experience the wonderful light that was lit when Jesus appeared in the world. In light I have hope, a new beginning! Jesus was and is a light to the world. Only as I understand the darkness in which I once lived can I fully comprehend and experience the wonderful light of Jesus.

Today I have hope as I rejoice in the light of the world, Jesus Christ!

❦

DECEMBER 18   GREED

*"Take care! Be on your guard against all kinds of
greed; for one's life does not consist in the abundance
of possessions."*
                                        —Luke 12:15

My greed often results from my need to
divert stressful feelings by indulging in compulsive behavior. A never-ending cycle of eat-
ing, working, or shopping takes the place of
seeking nurture in more healthy ways. As a
result I am saddled with unwanted pounds,
poor health, or bills I cannot pay. All of this
feeds my low self-esteem.

Today I will be free of greed that manifests
itself in compulsive ways of living. I see how
this behavior victimizes me and hurts the people I love. If I need help to work against these
feelings I will seek it. Others have admitted
and overcome their lack of self-control, and so
can I. By facing this dark side of myself I move
away from the sin of greed with dignity and
guiltlessness and take my place alongside others who also struggle.

**Today I seek the help and guidance I need to
overcome my greed and regain control of my
life.**

DECEMBER 19   SURRENDER

Then Mary said, "Here am I, the servant of the Lord; let it be with me according to your word."
—Luke 1:38

Mary, the mother of Jesus, was ready to see God work in her life. As she waited for the birth of Jesus, she lived in a time of expectation and surrender. Hers was not a passive surrender but one in which she continued to take action and live each day to the fullest.

Today I, too, surrender and take chances. I dare to see God work in my life. I take risks and even make some mistakes. I look forward to living today to its fullest.

Sometimes I feel as if I'm wearing armor to keep God and others at a distance in order to protect myself. But today I say, "Here I am Lord, your servant. May your purpose for my life be according to your will, and may we work together to achieve it!"

I surrender to God and take a chance today.

DECEMBER 20   *GIVING*

"But when you give a banquet, invite the poor, the crippled, the lame, and the blind. And you will be blessed, because they cannot repay you, for you will be repaid at the resurrection of the righteous."
—*Luke 14:13-14*

I am learning how to be a gracious, willing giver. My gift to another comes from my abundant wealth of self-assurance as a child of Christ, who is worthy of God's love. I have received life's bountiful gifts and, therefore, can share what I have received.

When I was a child I needed much more love than I received. I gave in the vain hope of getting something in return. But today I give as it is appropriate and needful. Giving is a loving act because I freely give by choice, with no strings attached.

I especially know the joy of giving when I share with others the good I have been given. My material gift shows my love, but more important, it points to the divine presence in the world who gave the greatest gift of all.

Today I give without expecting repayment.

The angel said to her, "Do not be afraid, Mary, for you have found favor with God."   —Luke 1:30

Mary was told by the angel not to be afraid. Rather than frantically wrestle with her dilemma she found peace, even in solitude, with her situation.

Like Mary, I am at peace, for I am learning to enjoy spending time with myself in solitude. I no longer search frantically for something to do just to fill up my time. I no longer am consumed by the fear of quiet and inactivity—afraid to face empty hours, evenings, or weekends.

I enjoy doing things by myself on my day off. My home is a haven where I am creative with my time. I've learned to accept and appreciate those downtimes when I can be alone with myself and ponder.

I am assured that God is always present with me. I silence the voices that tell me I'm wasting time and that feelings of loneliness will overtake me. I'm comfortable with being alone, and I remain at peace with myself. I use my time of solitude to revitalize and equip myself for the journey ahead.

In my times alone I find comfort, wholeness, and God.

DECEMBER 22   PRAYER

But Mary treasured all these words and pondered them in her heart.   —Luke 2:19

Today I, like Mary, step back to ponder the events of my life. I use a portion of my day to meditate and pray. Slowing my pace, I reconnect with God's wisdom working within my life. I take some time to think about my purpose, my direction, and the source of my being. I treasure time for thought and prayer.

At times when I feel overwhelmed with all the choices before me, I stop all that I'm doing to reflect on where I'm going. I do not let the uncertainty of tomorrow overshadow today. Neither do I let the promises of another day cause me to forget to enjoy today's possibilities.

As I slow down, I look around and observe what I'm doing and why I'm doing it. I am happy in the serenity and calm that my time of prayer and reflection brings. Guided by God's wisdom, I live today to its fullest and take tomorrow in stride.

I'm fully present in the moment as I take time to slow my pace, consider my actions, and talk with God.

DECEMBER 23   RELATIONSHIPS

Now the time came for Elizabeth to give birth, and she bore a son. Her neighbors and relatives heard that the Lord had shown his great mercy to her, and they rejoiced with her.   —Luke 1:57-58

Elizabeth had something wonderful happen in her life, and her friends and relatives rejoiced with her. They were happy that she got what she had wanted for so long.

Today I'm sorting out my relationships with a new awareness. I have a vision of what it means to be supportive of other people, and I am slowly making changes so that I may be present with others. In the past, I confused being supportive with smothering or intruding when uninvited. Sometimes I still cut myself off from other people in order to avoid smothering them.

Now I am redefining how I understand the intimacy of support. To support someone does not mean I have to be responsible for them or give up my identity so that they can feel valued and loved. Today I am supportive of my friends in full, rich, and realistic ways.

I support and rejoice with my friends and relatives.

DECEMBER 24   GOALS

And she gave birth to her firstborn son and wrapped him in bands of cloth, and laid him in a manger, because there was no place for them in the inn.
—Luke 2:7

Mary had a baby, wrapped the child in strips of cloth, and laid him in a feedbox to keep him safe. Steps that may seem insignificant were important to the beginning of Jesus' life. Some efforts may seem small and insignificant, yet each step is important when viewing the big picture.

In the past I was fearful that small steps weren't enough. I wanted to do things in BIG ways rather than accomplish small acts that would build toward my goals. I was also fearful that my best wasn't good enough. Many times I was not praised for the things I accomplished.

Now I realize I can't change the messages others choose to give me. Instead, I must change the messages I give myself. Today I remind myself that with each small step I take I'm one step closer to achieving my goals.

Today I take small steps to reach my goals.

And suddenly there was with the angel a multitude of the heavenly host, praising God and saying, "Glory to God in the highest heaven, and on earth peace among those whom he favors!" —Luke 2:13-14

I affirm the joy and glory of this day. Like the angels when Christ was born, I, too, praise God and delight in God's presence on earth. Every day I take time to delight in the passion of the day and to smile and laugh.

Laughter helps relieve the tension and rids my body of negative energy. Laughter fills me with happiness and joy. Laughter makes me glad to be alive.

There are days when life appears bleak and humorless. But I know I have the power to get up, brush myself off, and go on. I find that a smile on my face and laughter in my voice help me live through the absurd and comical inconsistencies of life. I chuckle at the ridiculous and keep on going.

I find joy in life, and my joy is reflected in my laughter and mirth.

Then an angel of the Lord stood before them, and the glory of the Lord shone around them, and they were terrified. But the angel said to them, "Do not be afraid; for see—I am bringing you good news of great joy for all the people."   —Luke 2:9-10

I celebrate this season of Christmas when I remember the birth of the Christ child. Because of Jesus, I have good news to live and share. I celebrate not only Christ's birth but also my own. I am thankful to be alive, and each day I have a clearer understanding of God's purpose for my life.

Just as the shepherds were guided by the angel, so also God guides me. Day by day I take steps to fulfill my purpose. What I do is important.

At times I worry that people won't like what I'm trying to accomplish. But, like the shepherds who heard the angel, I am reminded, "Do not be afraid; for see—I am bringing you good news of great joy for all the people." I remember and share the good news of God's purpose in my life.

In this season of Christ's birth I live my life's purpose boldly, knowing that it is God who guides me.

DECEMBER 27   JOY

*When they saw that the star had stopped, they were
overwhelmed with joy. On entering the house, they
saw the child with Mary his mother; and they knelt
down and paid him homage. Then, opening their
treasure chests, they offered him gifts of gold, frank-
incense, and myrrh.*

—*Matthew 2:10-11*

Today, like the wise men who found the
Christ child, I surrender myself to joy! I
release the tight reins I hold on my emotions
and discover the joy of this day.

When I give up full control, I free myself to
experience the moment. There is sheer delight
in living each experience, knowing I will not
be destroyed. If I do become unbalanced and
fall, I know I'll get back up, brush myself off,
and go on.

Extending myself to others in joy is my goal
today. The gifts I give may not be gold, frank-
incense and myrrh, but they may be gifts of
humor, wisdom, and love. These are the most
generous and joy-filled gifts I can give.

I free myself to experience the joy of this day!

❦

DECEMBER 28   THANKFULNESS

I will give thanks to you, O LORD, among the peoples, and I will sing praises to you among the nations. For your steadfast love is higher than the heavens, and your faithfulness reaches to the clouds.
—*Psalm 108:3-4*

I am thankful that in the midst of this chaotic world I am centered in God's steadfast love and faithfulness. I give thanks to God that

❦ I am making choices beyond survival.
❦ I am motivated by love, not fear.
❦ I am able to have fun, relax, and enjoy life.
❦ I am moving on to perfection without having to be perfect.
❦ I am growing and changing.
❦ I am able to set limits and say no when necessary.
❦ I am allowed to feel sadness and joy.
❦ I am on a journey to total healing.

Today I thank God for helping me on my journey.

DECEMBER 29 SELF-ACCEPTANCE

I praise you, for I am fearfully and wonderfully made. —Psalm 139:14a

"Beauty is in the eye of the beholder." I see myself and know that I am beautiful! It's wonderful to accept myself as I am.

Advertisements tell me I'm too fat or too thin, too tall or too short. This used to bother me, but now I set all these comparisons aside. I'm satisfied with who I am.

People tell me how to dress for success or for their approval. Starting today I dress the way I want to. I choose clothes that fit my personality and feel good to me. I am free to express who I am. Beauty is in the eye of the beholder—and I like what I see.

I praise God who has made me wonderfully beautiful!

DECEMBER 30   ACCEPTANCE

Praise the LORD! Sing to the LORD a new song, his praise in the assembly of the faithful. —Psalm 149:1

Today I sing a new song, for I am learning to accept and live in reality: the reality of my feelings, the reality of other people, and the ultimate reality of God's will. I am in a process of "reality-based" living.

One of the most important pieces I bring to this process is my past. My past life experiences are now an integral part of me. Painful events I have experienced are now a part of the weave. I am filled with wisdom as I accept and integrate my pain of the past and my hope for the future into my present reality.

With each passing year I become more fully myself. When I accept reality, everything in my life readily falls into place.

Today I sing a new song as I live fully in reality.

DECEMBER 31   TRANSITION

But these are written so that you may come to believe that Jesus is the Messiah, the Son of God, and that through believing you may have life in his name.
—John 20:31

I feel deep satisfaction as I think about the past year, and I feel great anticipation as I look forward to the new year. In this in-between time I pause and survey my life. I'm happy with what I see. I am more disciplined and, therefore, more liberated. I am more accepting and giving and, therefore, more peaceful. I have more grace for myself and, therefore, more love for others.

With each day that dawns, I fearlessly look for the new opportunities and inspiring ways Christ works through my life. I've faced some intense difficulties these past twelve months, but each time I have come out stronger and more powerfully filled with the Holy Spirit. Most important, God has given me the wisdom I have needed.

Joyously I open the door to the new year and walk through!

With God by my side, I'm ready, willing, and able to take the giant leap into tomorrow.

——— INDEX ———

NOTES

NOTES

NOTES